TABLE OF

Foreword

For over 6 years, Marc has been promoting and championing the tradition and camaraderie of the home game. Beginning as Marc's Small Stakes poker in 1998, he built a landing pad for would be players who wanted some kitchen table action. And just like the home game, a family was soon created. Marc found the internet to be alive with players discussing the game, the bad beats and the oddball variants from different states and countries, so much tradition being exchanged from different players around the world. Over time, contributions from many sources around the world enriched the scope of HomePoker.com.

When I was invited to join him in 2002, to aid in reaching even more home players, I was elated. Our plan was simple, make sure that anyone who wants to learn how to play poker at home, or who needs anything to get started can get it from us. When we were contacted by BradyGames to publish this work, we felt we were approaching a milestone. The game of poker in any environment can be intimidating for some, but in the home every effort should be made for as inviting an atmosphere as possible. For the player who's still working up the nerve to the player who just wants to know a little more to round out their experience, we have made an effort here to compile the how-to on some of poker's most popular games as well as variants of the more obscure. I hope that you enjoy this collection and that it adds to the environment of your own home game.

Sincerely,

Joel Krass

HomePoker.com

PREPARING YOUR HOME GAME

While a game can break out at any time where there's a deck of cards, a healthy atmosphere lends a great deal to your game experience. When you're ready to stop playing for change on a stack of dictionaries or lumber, you might want to invest in your game's ambiance with a set of chips, or a table. If you're planning a poker night around another event, like the Superbowl, or any big game, make sure to provide enough atmosphere to keep up the energy. There are a number of ways that you can help to make sure that you have an evening that's as fun as it is memorable.

Ring Poker vs. Tournament Poker

While tournament poker has been the staple of professional poker play for decades, it has only recently made its way into the home game. The home game has typically been characterized by the ring game format. What follows is a discussion of the two types of the differences between the two game formats and what you can expect from tournament poker.

Ring Game Poker

In the ring game, stakes are specified in advance but players show up with as much money as they want as a buy-in. If, for example, the night of poker is played with quarter antes and one dollar maximum raises, players may show up with anywhere from $20 to $50. Hands are dealt over and over again, with each player winning some hands and losing other hands. Your bankroll moves up and down from hand to hand. You get up and leave the table whenever you feel like going home, and when you do so, you take as much money as you still have in front of you. Games are usually called by the dealer, and the session ends when there are no players willing to continue playing.

Tournament Poker

Tournament poker is structured much differently. For starters, the buy-in is set in advance. Instead of players showing up with as much money as they care to gamble, they show up with a set amount if they want to buy into the tournament. If the buy-in is $50, then players need to submit $50 to the host if they want to play in the tournament. It's not flexible, it's the ticket amount for each player that wants in. You can play a tournament for $5 or $500, so don't feel that a low stakes ring game won't allow for it.

Just like a ring game, your bankroll moves up and down, but instead of being able to get up and leave whenever you want, there are only three ways you're leaving the tournament. Either you are eliminated from the tournament, you forfeit your seat, or you win the tournament. For your buy-in, you receive a set amount of chips. It's the same set amount that each other player in the tournament receives. The game is played, and when a player runs out of chips, he or she is out of the tournament. The other participants continue to play. Obviously, the number of players who remain in the tournament decreases as the tournament progresses. What started out as a tournament of 15 players, for example, dwindles down to eventually two players. Those are the last two survivors in the game and have all of the tournament's chips split between the two of them. They continue to play until one of them holds all of the tournaments chips, the other player is the runner-up.

PREPARING

BASICS

DRAW

STUD

GUTS

COMMUNITY

HOLD'EM

CASINO

NON-POKER

GLOSSARY

3

This is the foundation of tournament poker. Each player receives a set amount of chips and players are eliminated from the tournament as they run out of chips. From there, your tournament can be customized however you see fit, but at its base, every tournament functions along these lines. There are two important distinctions that tournament poker draws from regular ring-games: 1) that players know exactly how much they stand to lose, and 2) that nobody will win some money, and leave when they are satisfied with their winnings. In tournament poker, you either win the tournament or you don't. There are obviously some other subtleties with tournament poker that will be noted right off the bat.

First of all, there are many more losers. In hosting the tournament, you may decide that only the winner is awarded any money. Alternately, you may determine (like the World Series of Poker) that the top few players split the money. For example, first place may win 70% of the total purse, with 20% going to second place, and 10% going to third place. Even with such a format, there will only be 1-3 players who leave the game with any money. In regular play, it is feasible for everybody to leave with approximately what they started with, or for one player to win modestly while everybody else suffers a small loss. In tournament play however, the first-prize finisher wins most of the money, and if there are second and third-prize winners, they split what's left. Most of the players go home having lost their buy-in.

The bad news is that many players like the notion of going home with some, if not all, of their money. Tournament play has a winner-take-all attitude that may not necessarily be welcomed by all home poker players. Also, the notion of the tournament seems to be a little too serious for some players who prefer the friendly nature of the regular ring game. The good news is that a big purse puts a weight on the game that a ring game can't. When players get hot early, they'll be thinking of how they're going to spend that meaty purse, while in the late stages, every hand can be a heartbreaker as chip leads are won and lost and players are eliminated. The tournament is far more exciting than a regular ring game could ever be. Yes, fewer players go home with money, but it's a slobber-knocker of a game until that point. It's as fun as regular ring game poker could ever be, but it forces players to bring their best game to the table. Further, some players actually prefer knowing that their loss is limited to the buy-in. In other words, there's no worry of one's wallet ending up on the table. If the tournament buy-in is $50, then $50 is the most that a player can lose. That can be reassuring for some players.

Cards

As cards get passed around the table, dropped, spilled on, bent, burned and so on, they get marked. Nothing kills a game like not having usable cards. If you're hosting a serious game, or one with the potential to get serious, you need to have at least 2 decks of cards handy. If you can, make one red and one blue to prevent others from stacking hands, whether by accident or intentionally. If you play a tournament game, and would like to keep the game moving, have the player ahead of the dealer shuffle the cards for the next hand to reduce the downtime between play.

It is only a matter of time before you wear out a deck of cards. If you play often, good quality cards are inexpensive on the internet and can be ordered by the dozen for under $20.

Poker Chips

It seems like a big step to move away from nickel/dime poker to playing with chips, but it really completes the

PREPARING

BASICS

DRAW

STUD

GUTS

COMMUNITY

HOLD'EM

CASINO

NON-POKER

GLOSSARY

DEALER

5

experience. Not just in the look and feel, but in the economy of not actually taking home a hat full of loose change. If you're wondering how many chips you need, a set of 300 is fine for a small group of 5 - 6 in a standard ring game. If your group is bigger, or if you plan to play tournaments, a set of 500 is suitable for 8 - 10 players.

The cheapest upgrade from change is plastic chips. These are available at most department stores and game shops, they're cheap and they do the trick for under $20.

CHIP COLOR AND QUANTITY

As far as colors of chips are concerned, it's your game, so you can choose which ever you want. For those who are casino-minded, the general rankings of casino chips are white $1, red $5, green $25, blue $50, black $100.

For a 300 chip selection, a good split is 100 white, 150 red, 50 black. On a 500 chip set, go with 200 white, 200 red, 100 green, 50 blue, 50 black.

If you're looking for something more upscale than the plastic chip, the best place to shop for chips is the internet. Until very recently, poker chips have not been given much profile in retail stores. You can find all kinds of poker chips online and the prices are competitive. The price on chip sets range between $40 - $200 depending on your tastes, but the 8.6g diamond chip is a great value priced item that is perfect for a family game on a family budget. Most chips are made of a composite resin surrounding a metal disc. Some incorporate a higher percentage of clay, giving them a softer feel and more authentic weathering. It's all reflected in the cost. The closer you want your chips to be of the quality of casino chips, the more you're going to pay per chip.

Prices range from $0.09 per chip to $1.25 for a customized, pure clay chip.

Distributing Chips

Before you start spreading out chips between players, you should first determine whether the night's gaming allows for players to cut their losses and run, or for it to continue until one player is left with all the chips.

The easiest way to hold any poker game is to have players purchase chips and to cash them out at the end of a game. If your game is going to be a tournament, this is easy. Just divide the chips into equal amounts for each player. If you plan to allow players to rebuy into your tournament, leave about 10 - 15% of your total chips aside for players to buy back in if they lose early. For example, if you have 500 chips of different colors and want to have a four man Hold 'Em tournament, just give each player 125 chips and start the game. Players can agree on a tournament buy-in, and you play until one player has all the chips. If you want to allow for rebuys in the preceding example, give each player 100 chips, then leave 100 for players to buy back in.

If you're running a ring game, you can just have players buy in and cash out as they please. Set your chip colors to denominations that fit your limits and take cash on par. If your minimum bet is going to be $.25, that's the lowest chip you need. For example, on a $20 buy-in at a quarter ante game, consider 30 white chips (valued at $.25), 15 red chips (valued at $.50), and 5 black chips (valued at $1). This gives each player a good number of small bets and big bets to start the night off right. How you set your denominations is wholly determined by what you have available. If you have 3 chip colors, use a sort of small, medium,

PREPARING

BASICS

DRAW

STUD

GUTS

COMMUNITY

HOLD'EM

CASINO

NON-POKER

GLOSSARY

and large in a relation of 1:2:4 or 1:2:5. Just keep them as even multiples of the smallest bet or ante at your table and things will work themselves out. Use the bulk of the chips you have available, but remember to keep some aside in case players who run out want to get back into the game.

Remember to make the buy in reasonable, not too high or too low for your friends. You don't want to alienate people, or future games might end up shorthanded. You are the best judge of your crowd, so take their spending habits into consideration when suggesting a buy-in.

If you're worried about your game running over time, the plug can be pulled on a ring game at any time. If you need everyone out at 11:00, make it known at the beginning of the night and let people know that you'll be shutting things down an hour or so before. There will be no guilt about late luck if people know they can't play until dawn to get their money back. If you're playing a tournament, double your minimums every hour or more to speed up the action. If it's still too slow, add an ante, and speed up the chip bleed on players who aren't winning hands.

Table or Felt

Any flat surface can be used to play poker. A flipped over cardboard box or old fruit crate to a green baize table with a padded rail. If you have the space and the funds, some beautiful tables can be found online for wholesale prices.

For the student or family game, a cheap option to upgrade your playing surface is a simple 36 x 72 inch Blackjack or Craps felt. These are easily found on the internet for about $15, and make the conversion to a non poker game easy. Additionally, Craps is a great game for a group when you want a break from cards.

One step up from a felt is a folding table top. These are rigid surfaces usually with spring loaded chip trays and drink holders on each position. You can usually find these with 6 or 8 player positions. Folding tops are felt covered, and fold in half to fit in a storage and carrying case. They are available for about $60 - $80 depending on the model.

Folding leg card tables are a great option for the regular group of players who want to enjoy a high quality game experience at home without investing a whole room to do it. You can find these tables online in many finishes and sizes for about $200 - $300.

If you really want to capture the casino experience at home, a top of the line, full-size casino poker table with a dealer position, plunger and chip tray can be bought for about a thousand dollars, dealer not included. Similar models with folding legs are much less expensive, although still dear at $400. For any folding leg table, purchasing online means shipping will be expensive.

Cigars

For some, nothing completes the home poker experience like the blue smoke of a cigar wafting in an opponents face while contemplating a bluff. Paul Stulac, of Halifax's Smoke on the Water and CigarGangster.com, was asked for advice on choosing the best cigars for the home card player. Of course, he said get Cubans but it didn't stop there.

Paul also revealed a trade secret; all the major cigar manufacturers release lower priced bundled cigars. These are unbanded (the

PREPARING

BASICS

DRAW

STUD

GUTS

COMMUNITY

HOLD'EM

CASINO

NON-POKER

GLOSSARY

band is the paper wrapped around the end of the cigar) factory seconds in bundles of 20 or 25 for a discounted price. Often you can find a high quality cigar for only a few dollars per cigar. While these are not the same quality of the regular banded cigars, for the price they far exceed the cigars in the $2 or $3 price class. There's no fancy packaging here, just a cellophane wrap. Get yourself one of the same brand, take off the band, and your buddies will never know that you're smoking the real deal while they puff on the subs.

Currently hot brands are Gurkha or Graycliff. Gurkas are available for as low as $7 - $20 each, while Graycliff cigars are slightly more expensive. For the smoker who wants a smooth-flavored cigar that is comparatively easy on the pocket book, Paul highly recommends these two brands. Paul Stulac's own brand will available in the US and Canada in 2005, and range from mild to full bodied flavor for the casual smoker to the true aficionado.

You'll want to make sure that your cigars are fresh, so store your cigars in a humidor before your game or buy them as close to your poker night as possible. Humidors are best kept at 70% humidity and 70^0 F. They are available on line, or at your local retailer. If you do purchase online, don't worry about your cigars arriving stale. CigarGangster offers guaranteed delivery within 7 - 10 days of ordering, in sealed packaging with guaranteed freshness. If you're not satisfied, you can return your purchase, or receive a replacement with no questions asked.

You can find more information on choosing the perfect cigar, or order online at www.cigargangster.com or at www.paulstulac.com.

Food

If you're looking to host a game, and you think the guests might be hungry, you should keep people fed if you expect the game to keep any kind of pace. Any kind of food that can be left to be eaten when people get hungry works the best. A pot of meatballs set to simmer with a few fresh kaiser rolls and grated cheese makes an easy sandwich buffet. Lasagna is a good fit as well. If your group doesn't like Italian, a sandwich or taco bar lets players serve themselves. If you can't work a stove, maybe you can work a grill. A grill full of burgers and hot dogs should easily feed the army of starving gamblers at your game. At the HoldemMainia tournaments, the first player out is the designated grill master. If you can't work a barbeque or stove, you can likely work a phone. Pizza is a great option, as most folks will eat it in just about any state and it feeds a group well.

Music

Many players have written claiming that tells become extremely evident when players are grooving to their favorite ditty, but that's dependent on the player. For those that are not more partial to their tunes, they may betray a good hand if they start to move to the beat. Take it as you will, but a little music can help keep the mood fresh.

Etiquette

For some, the fear of making a Miss Manners type of error is harder to face than a bad beat. These players are as worried about offending other players or friends as they are of embarrassing themselves. An honorable lot, this section is for them. There are a few rules of etiquette that may not be apparent to players

PREPARING

BASICS

DRAW

STUD

GUTS

COMMUNITY

HOLD'EM

CASINO

NON-POKER

GLOSSARY

instinctively, and they're listed below. Remember that these are not law, some tables are more concerned with these types of rules than others and situations may call for a rule of etiquette to be ignored.

The best way to avoid problems is to make the rules of conduct as clear as possible before the first card is dealt. Doing so won't solve every problem, but it should help reduce the number of misunderstandings that lead to disagreements. Use your discretion.

1. Table Talk

If you're at a new table, keep the commentary down. You should get a feel for how much talk is too much fairly quickly. If you're not in the hand, it's a safe bet to keep your mouth shut. If you are in the hand, some players make chirping a big part of their game. Is it tasteful? That's a matter of opinion. Does it work? Amarillo Slim made a career of it. One anecdote relates Slim playing a notable women's champion in three separate contests. He beat her the first two times armed with lewd barbs (and a lifetime of poker acumen); the third she came to the game with a walkman on and tuned out ol' Slim all the way to victory. That woman was Betty Carrey.

2. Playing against the other blind

In Texas Hold 'Em, if only the blind bets are in the hand, they have the option to pull their bets back and the deal moves to the next player. There have been cases where players have been pressed on this and elected to play the hand in the face of bad etiquette. Could it happen again? Probably not with Six, Eight offsuit, but it's difficult to lay down a big hand, despite manners. Few players would expect anyone to lay day a monster, particularly in a tournament situation.

3. Requesting to see mucked cards

If you're playing Hold 'Em, and you ask the dealer to see the hand that a player has mucked, you are accusing her or him of collusion. No matter your intent, when you ask a dealer to dig a hand out of the muck, you are accusing a player of colluding with another player to beat you. Be sure if you're going to do this. Many players incorrectly use this rule to gain information about an opponent's habits. While you are technically allowed to pull hands out of the muck, this in is the poorest of poor taste.

4. Dine and Dash

No one likes a player who wins big and suddenly has other commitments. While this is fine in a casino, it's not acceptable in the home game. If you fleece your friends, at least give them some sort of opportunity to win a portion of that money back (not all of it though!) That's not to say that you have to stay until you're cleaned out, but at least stay long enough for the deal to go around before you decide to make your exit.

5. Showing Cards

In Texas Hold 'Em, only the player who intends to win a contested hand must show cards. If two players showdown, and one can see his or her hand is beat, he or she may muck that hand. However, this is not the case in many home variations. Depending on the game, players usually will showdown, and not muck. The amount of deception and the degree to which it is enforced is specific on your own home. If you do not wish to allow players to muck hands on a final betting round that is your prerogative. Most of the home variations listed have players rolling their hands at showdown at the same time. In Hold 'Em, showing your mucked hand is a courtesy to the table. In most home games, it's a requirement. Players who fold, of course, do not need to reveal their cards.

PREPARING

BASICS

DRAW

STUD

GUTS

COMMUNITY

HOLD'EM

CASINO

NON-POKER

GLOSSARY

Further Reading

If you're looking to further your knowledge of poker there are a number of great resources that can provide in-depth instruction on taking your game to the next level. The following titles are some of the most widely read titles in the poker world.

The Theory of Poker, David Sklansky
This is THE book on poker theory. If you want to understand the way that the mathematically and statistically inclined pros think, this is a must read. If you're a more intuitive player, you should still read this, if not only to gain understanding as to what is happening on the other side of the baize. There are few books with this sort of depth, and few authors with this sort of credit. In many ways, Sklansky's works define how to properly play the game of poker at an elite level.

Hold 'Em Poker, David Sklansky
If you're planning to play casino Hold 'Em or want to take your home Hold 'Em game up a notch, check out this book. Sklansky breaks down the importance of position, hole cards, flops, reading hands and more. A must for the serious Hold 'Em player.

Hold 'Em Poker for Advanced Players,
David Sklansky, Mason Malmuth
This book takes Sklansky's earlier Hold 'Em Poker book one step further. It contains updated information about the changes in the game that have come about through new structures in card rooms, as well as improvements to strategy when playing expert players. This work is for the well-disciplined, experienced players who are interested in improving their work on semi-bluffing, drawing hands, playing trash, fourth street and much more. This is a text for would-be experts by the authorities of the game.

Winning Low Limit Hold 'Em, Lou Kreiger

Mr. Kreiger lays out a formula for tight, aggressive casino play that is very effective at low-limits. By remaining disciplined, you will get ahead using Lou's method. His lessons are ideal for the no fold 'em Hold 'Em play from $2/$4 to $5/$10. Be warned however, if you are an advanced player, or play at high limits, Krieger admits that this book is not for you. The author of this article uses many of Lou's techniques whenever possible. His system is sound; it is the discipline of the player that is questionable.

Thursday Night Poker, Peter O. Steiner

Intended for the biweekly or monthly poker player, Steiner breaks down calculating probabilities, estimating odds, bluffing, reading hands and more. This is a well illustrated and clearly written book.

The Rules of Neighborhood Poker According to Hoyle, Stewart Wolpin

One of the few books devoted purely to the home game, Wolpin discusses in detail the politic of proper behavior of the home game as well as the rules of game. The focus here is for the casual home player.

Big Deal, A Year as a Professional Poker Player, Anthony Holden

This is not a book on strategy or how to play at home. Rather it is the account of Holden's decision to leave his job as a journalist to pursue a career as a professional card player. His exchanges with poker greats Johnny Moss, Slim Preston and more make for a book of poker mystique and magic that can't be put down by even the non-card player. Will it help your game? Probably not. Will it entertain and educate you on the substance and history of the poker world. Most definitely.

PREPARING

BASICS

DRAW

STUD

GUTS

COMMUNITY

HOLD'EM

CASINO

NON-POKER

GLOSSARY

POKER BASICS

Home poker takes the concept of card playing for money and combines it with friendly spirit, low risks and rewards (even for the night's losers and big winner), and a variety of different game formats. Some of these variations stray so far off that the only criteria appears to be that there be cards involved, and a sum of money on the line.

Home poker places less emphasis on money-making, and is more a social game. By contrast, what's played in Las Vegas is a more cut-throat, winner-take-all contest. The gambling element of home poker is still present. The amounts of money are not the same, but home poker is still a game where a dollar is a bluff.

Covered in the following pages are the basic principles of home poker. Most of what is found here are poker rules written in stone, no matter who is playing or what stakes are. As you will learn when you play from table to table, no two groups play home poker identically. These are the conventions that are adopted by tables, dealing with similar situations in different ways.

This section is suitable for people who do not know anything about poker as well as those who know the game, but need a refresher.

What Beats What

The following is the hierarchy of poker hands, from worst to best. Poker changes from one table to the next, but the following is indisputable:

PREPARING

BASICS

DRAW

STUD

GUTS

COMMUNITY

HOLD'EM

CASINO

NON-POKER

GLOSSARY

High card

If you do not have anything in your hand, then your best hand is the highest card in your hand. For example, King-high means that nothing in your hand matches with anything else, and the King is the highest card in your hand.

Pair

Two of your cards are the same, like 2 Jacks.

Two Pairs

Your hand includes two different pairs, like 2 Eights and 2 Tens.

Three-of-a-Kind

Three of your cards are the same.

Straight

All five of your cards are in numerical sequence, regardless of the suits of the cards.

Flush

All five of your cards are the same suit. They do not have to be in any sequence, but they must be of the same suit.

Full House

This is a combination of a pair and a three-of-a-kind.

Four-of-a-Kind

Four of your cards are the same.

Straight Flush

All five of your cards are the same suit and all in sequence.

TIE-BREAKERS

If two or more players at the table share a similar winning hand, then use the following tie-breakers to determine a winner.

For Pairs, Three-of-a-Kind and Four-of-a-Kind, the higher matched cards beat the lower matched cards. If two players hold the same Pair (without wildcards, it's impossible for two players to have the same Three-of-a-Kind or Four-of-a-Kind), then the highest remaining cards in each hand are compared.

For Two Pair, the highest paired cards win the hand. If the players hold identical high Pairs, then the player holding the higher second Pair wins. If both players hold the same Two Pairs, then their fifth cards are compared with the higher card winning the hand.

The tie-breaker for Full Houses is to compare each hand's Three-of-a-Kind with the higher cards winning.

For Straights, Flushes and Straight Flushes, compare the highest card used to make the Straight or Flush.

There will be times when all of these tie-breaking methods fail to produce a single winner. In these rare cases, the pot is split between the players with the identical hands.

Knowing the ranking of hands is a large chunk of the game, but knowing it by heart comes with time. If you're new to poker, either write down the sequence of winning hands, or look for a deck of cards that comes with an extra card that explains the ranking of poker hands. The sequence of betting rounds in a game is difficult to master but relatively simple to learn. The different types of games played require time to learn but are still easily categorized. The table of what beats what, however, is a big step towards understanding poker. You can follow a round of betting by watching it. You can learn a poker game by listening to the rules or watch it being played. However, this isn't worth much until knowing what will happen when all players throw down their hands to determine who wins.

The rankings of hands is no accident; it is based on the frequency with which these hands appear over time. For every 1000 hands of regular five card draw poker dealt, the distribution of hands should appear like this:

PREPARING

BASICS

DRAW

STUD

GUTS

COMMUNITY

HOLD'EM

CASINO

NON-POKER

GLOSSARY

NO PAIR	503 TIMES
ONE PAIR	422 TIMES
TWO PAIRS	47 TIMES
THREE-OF-A-KIND	21 TIMES
STRAIGHT	3.9 TIMES
FLUSH	1.9 TIMES

What's important to keep in mind about this information is that it's based on the mathematical laws of probability. When people get together to play a few rounds of poker, you're dealing with real outcomes, and anything is possible.

What's The Game

There are a variety of ways to play poker. There are silly games like Chase the Ace and Bing Bang Bong. There are more challenging games like Pass the Trash or Five-Card Draw. There are also the serious games played by professionals, like Texas Hold 'Em or Seven-Card Stud. All of these games are unique and fun in their own way.

When you are playing in a home poker game, the first question to answer is whether the same poker variant will be dealt over and over again all night, or, as is more often the case, Dealer's Choice is used. In Dealer's Choice, the deal rotates in clockwise order around the table. When it is a new dealer's turn, that player decides which of the variants of poker will be played. After declaring the game that will be played, players signal their agreement to play the game by putting their ante in the pot.

This method of playing poker is by far the most entertaining. It allows the table to play a great variety of games and to experiment with some new ones. Once you have been playing poker with the same group for long enough, some games will become mainstays at your table; the ones that everybody enjoys playing.

Wild Cards

Some of you are already familiar with the concept of wild cards from other card games. If you are going to be playing the same game over and over all night, then you will have already determined if there are wild cards. If you are playing Dealer's Choice, then it will be at the dealer's discretion to determine if there are wild cards, and if so, what they are.

The type of card that is wild must be specified. The dealer may determine that all Twos in the deck are wild, or all face cards in the deck are wild, or heaven forbid, that all Spades in the deck are wild. The point is that the dealer assigns wild card status to some identifiable denomination of cards.

The definition of a wild card is a card that can be used as any other specific card in the deck. For example, if Twos are wild and you have one in your hand, you can make that Two any card you want. Ideally, you would make it a card that helps complement the rest of your hand. If Twos are wild and your hand is:

then you have three "natural" Aces and a wild card (the Two of Spades). Since the Two is wild, you can decide that it is a fourth Ace in your hand, giving you four Aces instead of just three Aces.

The word natural is used to describe a card that is not wild. When you are using a card as it is and not as a wild card, it is said to be natural.

Bear in mind when you are playing wild card games that the more wild cards there are in a game, the more luck that is required to win. A game with no wild cards calls on significantly more skill than a game with plenty of wild cards. When the game has many wild cards, the winner is usually the player who was simply been dealt the most wild cards.

Getting Started– Stakes and First Deal

So, you're sitting at a table with five of your friends and a deck of cards. What next? The first thing that must be determined are the stakes. How much money is everybody willing to play for?

The basic way of defining stakes is answering the following questions:

1) **What will the standard ante be?**
2) **What is the minimum bet that a player can make?**
3) **What is the maximum bet that a player can make?**

The table's minimum bet defines just how low the stakes are. If the table's minimum bet is a nickel, then there are obviously no pennies allowed on the table. In this case, at no point could anything less than a nickel be placed as a bet.

The table's maximum bet defines just how high the stakes are. No player, in the course of a betting round, can bet anything higher than the table's maximum bet. If it is defined as fifty cents, then no more than fifty cents can be bet by a player.

PREPARING

BASICS

DRAW

STUD

GUTS

COMMUNITY

HOLD'EM

CASINO

NON-POKER

GLOSSARY

Within these two denominations is the range of money that can be bet by individual players throughout the course of the night.

The next thing to determine is who is going to deal the first hand. One way is by dealing out cards face-up to each player until a black-colored Jack turns up. The player who gets it calls the first game of the night. This is not extremely important, as some tables determine that the host of the night deals the first game.

What follows is a comprehensive breakdown of the different types of Home Poker games. For now, assume you are the dealer and you have selected a game. You would explain what the game is, await everybody's antes and begin dealing the cards.

Ante

The ante is a vital part of the poker game. The ante is a token amount of money that ensures that each player already has some stakes in the game being played.

When the dealer calls the game of his or her choice, every player is prompted to throw the predetermined ante into the pot. The ante is typically the same amount of money as the minimum table bet, and typically remains the same throughout the course of the night for every game.

It is not much money, but ensures that if a player folds immediately, that player has already lost some amount of money in this game.

The ante should be thought of as that small bit of interest that keeps every player involved in every game from the start. Before you even have cards dealt to you, you have already spent some money on this game. In other words, no looking at your cards and folding without already having lost some money.

The ante is also each player's signal that they understand the game that has been called and agree to play it. A player who does not ante is signaling that he or she is not interested in playing the particular game called by the dealer.

PREPARING

BASICS

DRAW

STUD

GUTS

COMMUNITY

HOLD'EM

CASINO

NON-POKER

GLOSSARY

Betting

Here's one scenario of how a betting round may go. You're at a table with five other players in a game of Five Card Draw. Player A, sitting to the left of the dealer, opens the betting round for a quarter. Player B sees the quarter. Player C sees the quarter and raises it another quarter. Player D sees the two quarters and calls. You see the two quarters and bump it another two quarters. The dealer folds. Player A sees the three quarters and raises a quarter. Players B and C fold. If Player D sees and calls, how much do you owe? The answer follows.

Betting goes in sequence. The player who opens the betting round is determined in the rules of the game, or otherwise is opened by the player sitting to the left of the dealer. Opening the betting round involves starting the round of betting with a sum of money. A player, however, has the option to say "no bet," meaning he or she is not interested in opening the betting round with a sum of money. The option then moves to the player to his or her left, and continues in clockwise order. When the betting round reaches a player, that player has no more than 3 options.

See the bet and call.
This means that the player matches what has been bet before him or her, and does not raise that amount at all.

See the bet and raise.
That player chooses to see, or match, all of the bets that have been made before him or her, and raises, or bumps, the bet with more money, making it more expensive for others who want to stay in the game.

Fold.

Simple enough. The player decides that the amount of bet money that has reached him or her is not worth it based on the hand he or she is holding. Players fold by putting their hand face-down, so nobody can see what cards you were holding, and not paying anything into the pot. That player does not stand to lose any more money in this game, but has also eliminated his or her chances of collecting the pot in the end.

Betting is a tactic used by players to do a number of things. If you have a good hand and are confident that you might win the pot, then increasing the amount of money that will be in the pot means more money added to your stack at the end of the hand. Another reason is that there are other players at the table who have lousy hands and are only staying in the game because it does not cost them anything. To eliminate such players from the game, a bet is made. This is often called keeping everybody honest.

Another reason to bet is that you have a horrible hand. Why bet with a horrible hand? This is called bluffing. The player knows, based on his or her hand, that there is no hope of winning, so he or she bets in order to scare other players out of the game by convincing them that his or her hand is much better than it really is. A player who bets high conveys the idea that he or she has a really good hand, and the hope of a bluffer is to scare off other players with this tactic.

To explain the previous betting scenario:

PLAYER A
Opens for a quarter. One quarter is on the line.

PLAYER B
Sees the quarter bet by Player A, and calls. One quarter still on the line.

PLAYER C
Sees the quarter bet by Player A, and bumps another quarter. Two quarters are on the line.

PLAYER D
Sees the two quarters bet by Players A and C, and calls. Two quarters are still on the line.

YOU
See the two quarters bet by Players A and C, and bumps another two quarters. Four quarters are now on the line.

DEALER
Folds. Four quarters are still on the line.

The betting round has made a full turn of the table, but there are still bets that have been made that other players owe on. Even though there were four quarters on the line, Player A does not need to match one of them, because it was from one of the bets that he had originally made.

PLAYER A
Sees the quarter bet by Player C and the two quarters bet by you, and bumps another quarter.

PLAYER B
Folds.

PLAYER C
Folds.

Unlike Player A, Player D has already seen the bet that was made by Player C. So...

PLAYER D
Sees the two quarters bet by you and the one quarter last bet by Player A, and calls.

If you said that you owe one quarter to stay in the game, you are correct. Since the last time that you bet, the only additional bet that was made was by Player A (note that everybody but the two of you and Player D have folded, and Player D did not bump the bet). Player A's bet was for a quarter, and that is what you owe to stay in the game.

The key to figuring out what you owe when the betting round gets to you is to calculate what bumps were made since the last time you bet, that is the amount of money that has been bet that you have yet to pay.

PREPARING

BASICS

DRAW

STUD

GUTS

COMMUNITY

HOLD'EM

CASINO

NON-POKER

GLOSSARY

Poker Game Categories
Draw Poker

Draw Poker involves each player being dealt a number of cards, followed by a betting round, followed by a draw. The draw allows each player to exchange a number of their cards for different cards from the deck that may better suit the player's hand. For example, a player who has three of five cards that are not doing anything to help his or her overall hand discards those three cards and is dealt three new cards from the deck. These are called blind cards, because a player does not know what they will be.

The dealer may designate "One draw of three cards," which means after the first betting round, players are allowed to exchange up to three cards from their hand for the same number of brand new cards from the deck.

This is the basic principle. Specifics are left to the dealer. For example, the dealer determines how many cards each player can exchange on the draw, as well as how many draws that will be allowed to each player (usually no more than three). Typically, the cards are dealt (usually five cards), followed by a betting round opened by the player to the left of the dealer, followed by the draw, followed by a final betting round.

Of course, this varies. The dealer may choose to allow 2 draws of a maximum of 2 cards per draw. In this case, there would be a betting round, a draw, another betting round, another draw, then the final betting round.

Draw Poker games can either be straight, meaning that there are no wild cards, or the dealer can determine that there are wild cards.

For example, in Deuces Wild, if a Two comes up in your hand, you can make it any card you want, to complement a Straight or Flush, or to turn a Three-of-a-Kind into a Four-of-a-Kind.

Stud Poker

The basic principle of Stud Poker games is that some of your cards are face-down, and only you are allowed to see them. The rest are face-up for everyone at the table to see. The point of this is that each player can see some of the cards in the other players' hands while having some cards of their own that nobody at the table can see.

The popular Stud Poker games are Seven-Card Stud and Five-Card Stud. Seven-Card Stud is dealt however the dealer decides, but the popular format is the initial 2 cards dealt face-down to each player, followed by 4 cards dealt face-up to each player, followed by the seventh card dealt face-down to each player. This is so that players can see how close other players may be to having, for example, a Flush or a Straight. The other, more fiendish purpose is for individual players to pretend they have better cards than they really do. For example, if the 4 face-up cards are the following:

then, the player can start betting high to convince the other players that a face-down card (in this case, the Six of Diamonds) is the one needed to complete the Straight Flush.

Poker hands consist only of 5 cards. In Seven-Card Stud, or any 7 card poker game for that matter, players make the best 5 card

PREPARING

BASICS

DRAW

STUD

GUTS

COMMUNITY

HOLD'EM

CASINO

NON-POKER

GLOSSARY

hand of the 7 cards before them. Three Pairs, for example, does not exist as a poker hand, even though you might have it in your hand. The player takes all seven cards and determines which five cards of those seven make up the best poker hand. The other two cards are ignored as the player calls his or her hand based on the best five cards.

Five-Card Stud is dealt along the same lines, some cards face-down and some face-up. The popular format is to initially deal one card face-down, followed by four cards face-up.

Although the specifics are left to the dealer, Stud Poker is typically played along the principle that the initial face-down cards are immediately dealt to each player, followed by one face-up card at a time. After each round of face-up cards are dealt, there is a betting round before the next round of face-up cards. These betting rounds are opened by the player who has the best hand showing of his or her face-up cards. For example, if there is a Pair of Eights showing, and no other player's face-up cards can beat that, then that hand opens the betting round.

Community Poker

No, it is not as friendly as it sounds. In fact, some people absolutely despise Community Poker games. This is the most flexible type of poker, the specifics left completely to the dealer.

The basic idea is that a number of cards are dealt to each player, after which the dealer lays out a certain number of cards in the middle of the table face-down. These cards are flipped over by the dealer one-by-one followed by a betting round after each community card is flipped. The purpose of these community cards is that they can be used in conjunction with each player's hand.

Guts Poker

In any game of Guts Poker, the players ante, are dealt their
hands, and decide whether or not they want to stay in the game.
Players that do not stay in the game are out until the next deal.
Of the players who stay in, the player with the best hand collects
the pot. The other players who went in must match the amount of
money that was in the pot when the round started. For example,
if 6 people are playing and ante a quarter each, there's $1.50 in
the pot. After cards are dealt, 4 players decide to go in. The other
two are out of the hand. The player of the four who has the best
hand at the end of the game collects the pot. The other 3 players
must each throw $1.50 into the pot. Now, there's $4.50 in the pot
and the same game is dealt again.

A Guts game keeps getting dealt over and over until one player
decides to go in. That one player collects the pot and the game
is over. So long as more than one player stays in after the deal,
at least one player must match the pot and the game continues.
Players do not have to go in if they do not want to risk having
to match the pot if they lose. However, a player who does not
stay in has no chance of collecting the pot.

PREPARING

BASICS

DRAW

STUD

GUTS

COMMUNITY

HOLD'EM

CASINO

NON-POKER

GLOSSARY

DRAW POKER

The basic premise behind Draw Poker is that all cards are dealt face-down to players, who have the option to change a certain number of the cards dealt to them for new cards from the deck. For many, this is the first style of poker learned, typically from Five Card Draw. In Five Card Draw, five cards are dealt to each player and in sequence; each has the option to exchange for new cards from the deck. Players try to improve the state of their hand by discarding those cards that add the least value.

The typical structure of a Draw Poker game is that cards are dealt to each player, followed by a betting round. Those players that get through the betting round are allowed a draw of cards from the deck. The draw is followed by another betting round, and then, showdown. Some players are accustomed to a draw before the first betting round. However, it is preferable to have a betting round before the draw so that players must first pay the price to get to the draw.

The dealer calling the game typically determines how many cards each player is allowed to draw. When making this decision, the dealer must ensure that enough cards are in the deck to allow each player their maximum draw. So be careful when calling a draw game when you have many players at your table. For example, a table of 10 people cannot play 5 card draw with a draw of even 1 card. In this scenario, a standard deck of cards only allows 2 players to draw before the dealer runs out of cards. Therefore, draw games are best suited for groups of 6-7 or less.

The dealer may call more than one draw. For example, five card draw with two draws of two cards. This would mean that players have two opportunities to exchange as many as two cards for new ones from the deck. An additional draw round means an additional betting round. In this case, there would be three betting rounds: one before the first draw, one in between the two draws, and the last after the second draw.

The number of cards that a player takes on the draw should also be used as one predictor of the player's hand. A player taking one card, for example, likely has Two Pair, or four cards to a Straight or Flush.

PREPARING

BASICS

DRAW

STUD

GUTS

COMMUNITY

HOLD'EM

CASINO

NON-POKER

GLOSSARY

♣♦♠♥ THE FEATURES ♣♦♠♥

The features that follow can be added to any Draw Poker game, including regular old Five Card Draw. Each is a variant on the game, thus creating a new game.

Through experience, you will find which features (if any) best suit the games most often played at your table.

Roll Your Own

The most common Draw Poker games involve wild cards determined in advance by the dealer. This variant allows players to determine what card they want to have wild in their hand. Obviously, if they have two or three cards that match, they will determine that that card is wild in their hand. For example, one low card and a Pair of Aces become three Aces.

Pay For Your Draw

This is a feature that is used to build the pot of any Draw Poker game. The dealer attaches a price to drawing a card. For example, the dealer determines that it costs one dollar for each card that a player wants to draw. A player drawing three cards must put three dollars into the pot on top of the amount accumulated from betting.

Leg Poker

This feature is more like two games in one. Most commonly played as double-legged poker, this variation requires that a player win the game twice before collecting the pot. The game plays as it normally would, except that when a player wins with the best hand, that player does not yet collect the pot. Instead, that player has earned a leg towards winning the pot. The pot remains in the center of the table, and the same game is dealt again, complete with betting rounds. The first player to win two legs wins the giant pot. A Three-Legged Race is triple-legged poker, where a player must win three legs before claiming the pot.

High/Low

This feature is split-pot poker, where the pot is split between two winning players. In High/Low, the pot is split between the player that has the best hand at the table, and the player that has the worst hand at the table. It is important to remember that when playing any high/low game that the table has the same opinion on what the best high or low hands are. There are many differing opinions of what the best low can be. Some tables don't count straights and flushes as low hands, others won't allow the Ace to be played low. When a high/low game is called, have the table agree on what is considered the best low hand. Most players allow an A-2-3-4-5 straight (the wheel) to be played low.

Lowball

This is "all-low poker." The worst hand at the table wins the pot. It is especially challenging in Draw Poker, where you may draw higher cards than the ones thrown away, or where you may accidentally pair up with one of the cards in your hand. Like High/Low poker, the qualifications for the lowest hand can change from region to region. Have the table agree on what's the lowest of the low to avoid arguments later.

Roll' Em

This is a feature that can be used to increase the number of betting rounds in a Draw Poker game. When players 'roll' their cards, they reveal them from their hand ONE CARD AT A TIME. After each player has shown a card from their hand to the rest of the table, a betting round follows opened by the player with the best hand showing. Players reveal their cards simultaneously so that there is no advantage gained. In this way, it is a Draw game being played like a Stud game.

New York Draw

Made popular by John Scarne, in this game, an outside Straight, that is four cards in numerical sequence without break, beats a Pair but loses to Two Pair. This variant offers (or is meant to offer) more reason to chase a straight.

Canadian Draw

This game plays the same as New York Draw, on top of which a Fourflush, that is four of your five cards are of the same suit, beats an outside Straight but loses to Two Pair. Therefore, the hierarchy of hands in this game is Pair, Outside Straight, Fourflush, Two Pairs. Evidently, Scarne believed that people in Canada play

PREPARING

BASICS

DRAW

STUD

GUTS

COMMUNITY

HOLD'EM

CASINO

NON-POKER

GLOSSARY

poker like this, of course they don't unless they're playing Canadian Draw.

Spanish Draw

This variation, which can be added to any poker game, means that all cards from Two through Six are removed from the deck. That means twenty cards out of play, and 32 cards remaining. Everything otherwise plays the same. If you're a player who calculates odds, change the base of your calculations from 52 to 32. That is, when trying to find out how many cards are available in the deck that can improve your hand, remember there are significantly fewer cards in the deck. So if you're sitting on a pair of Nines, there are 2 cards in 27 unseen cards (32 in the deck, less your hand of 5) giving you odds of basically 1-in-14 of improving your Nines. Usually, you have worse odds (2 cards in 47) for improving your pair. The scarcity of low cards makes big cards even bigger in Spanish game variations.

With A Qualifier

When a qualifier is added to a Draw Poker game, it means that for a player to open the betting round before the draw, that player must have a hand of minimum value determined by the dealer. For example, if the dealer determines that a pair of Jacks or better are required for a player to open the first betting round, then the player wishing to bet must show the other players at the table the cards from his hand that meet the qualifier. That player then returns the cards to his hand and opens the betting round. The betting round is followed by the draw. If no player has the qualifier, then nobody can open the first betting round, in which case the game is reset. That is, all cards are re-dealt and all players must ante again. This continues until somebody has the qualifier to open the first betting round. It is important to note that most tables do not allow players to bluff qualifiers to open or their qualifiers to take the pot. If a player has two Tens in Jacks or Better, Trips to Win, that player cannot bluff with Tens to get by the Jacks, and fold everyone with big bets to take the pot. If the game has a qualifier, the qualifier MUST BE MET!

With the Bug

This is a feature usually used for the entire night. In it, one Joker is put into the deck. That Joker is called 'the bug', but it has limited wild card value. It can only be used to complete a Straight or a Flush. Otherwise, it has no value. This would be stipulated as opposed to tables that play with Jokers as wild cards that have no limited wild card value and can be designated as any card to complete any hand.

PREPARING

BASICS

DRAW

STUD

GUTS

COMMUNITY

HOLD'EM

CASINO

NON-POKER

GLOSSARY

Basic Five Card Draw

The dealer must determine how many cards each player can exchange on the draw. If there are enough cards for all players, the dealer may decide that players can draw as many cards as they want. 5 cards are dealt face-down to each player. A betting round is opened by the player sitting to the left of the dealer. That player is "under the gun" for all betting rounds in the game, but can opt not to bet and check instead.

The betting round is followed by a draw, where players can exchange as many cards as were specified by the dealer. The draw begins with the player to the left of the dealer. The draw is followed by a second and final betting round. Those players remaining show down their 5 card hand.

5 CARD DRAW POKER

In 1000 deals of regular five card draw poker hands appear with the following frequency:

NO PAIR	503 TIMES	50.3
ONE PAIR	422 TIMES	42.2
TWO PAIRS	47 TIMES	4.7
THREE OF A KIND	21 TIMES	2.1
STRAIGHT	3.9 TIMES	0.39
FLUSH	1.9 TIMES	0.19

In a deck of cards, there are 2,598,960 available hands to be dealt

NUMBER IN DECK	HAND	ODDS OF HOLDING
40	straight flush	64973 to 1
624	four of a kind	4164 to 1
3744	full house	693 to 1
5108	flush	508 to 1
10200	straight	254 to 1
54912	three of a kind	46 to 1
123552	two pairs	20 to 1
1098240	one pair	1.25 to 1

Odds of improving your hand in a five card draw game

CARDS KEPT	# OF CARDS DRAWN	IMPROVED HAND	ODDS AGAINST
ACE	4	Pair	4 to 1
	4	three Aces	63 to 1
ACE WITH KING	3	Pair of Kings or Aces	3 to 1
ONE PAIR	3	Two Pair	5.25 to 1
	3	Three-of-a-Kind	8 to 1
	3	Full House	97 to 1
	3	Four-of-a-Kind	359 to 1
	3	Any improvement	2.5 to 1
PAIR WITH ACE	2	Two Pairs	8 to 1
	2	Three-of-a-Kind	12 to 1
TWO PAIR	1	Full House	11 to 1
THREE OF A KIND	2	Full House	15.5 to 1
	2	Four-of-a-Kind	22.5 to 1
OUTSIDE STRAIGHT	1	Straight	5 to 1
INSIDE STRAIGHT	1	Straight	11 to 1
FOUR FLUSH	1	Flush	4.5 to 1
THREE FLUSH	2	Flush	23 to 1
TWO FLUSH	3	Flush	96 to 1

PREPARING

BASICS

DRAW

STUD

GUTS

COMMUNITY

HOLD'EM

CASINO

NON-POKER

GLOSSARY

Acey Deucey

This game plays the same as Basic Five Card Draw, except that all Aces and Twos are wild cards. Players with one in their hand can designate that card as any card from the deck that best suits their hand. Having eight wild cards often leads to many big hands.

Stedman's (5s and 10s)

This game plays the same as Basic Five Card Draw, except that all Fives and Tens are wild cards. The game is named after the old chain of five and dime stores. Nowadays, you might hear this game referred to as WalMart or Target.

Snowmen and Hockey Sticks (8s and 7s)

This game plays the same as Basic Five Card Draw, except that all Sevens and Eights are wild cards. Like Stedmans and Acey Deucey, expect to see bigger hands appear from all the wild cards.

Pregnant Threes (3s, 6s and 9s)

This game plays the same as Basic Five Card Draw, except that all Threes, Sixes, and Nines are wild cards. This is twelve wild cards, folks. You either have four of a kind or you've stayed in the hand too long.

Heinz 57 (5s and 7s)

This game plays the same as Basic Five Card Draw, except that all Fives and Sevens are wild cards. Contrary to popular belief, when you play this game, John Kerry does not make a nickel.

Spit in the Ocean

Spit is a community draw game, where each player is dealt four cards. The dealer then flips a fifth card from the top of the deck. This card is the "spit" card, and makes up the fifth card in everyone's hand. There are several variations of Spit.

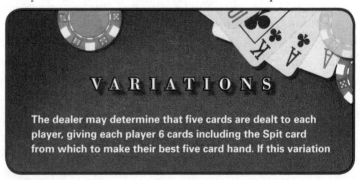

VARIATIONS

The dealer may determine that five cards are dealt to each player, giving each player 6 cards including the Spit card from which to make their best five card hand. If this variation

PREPARING

BASICS

DRAW

STUD

GUTS

COMMUNITY

HOLD'EM

CASINO

NON-POKER

GLOSSARY

is used, specify whether the Spit card must be used to complete the hand when calling this game.

Wild Widow

This is played as Spit in the Ocean, except that the Spit card and all matching cards in each player's hand are wild. The dealer may choose that the spit card itself is not wild, but that its three sister cards are wild. This is done to keep everyone from starting the game with at least one wild card.

Stormy Weather

Just edging on being a Community Poker Game, players are dealt their regular four cards and three community cards are dealt face-down. After the first betting round and draw, each community card is flipped over one at a time followed by a betting round. At showdown, players make their best five card hand with their four cards, and any **one** of the three community cards. Players **must use all four** of their dealt cards, and cannot play the entire board of three cards with two from their hand.

STRAIGHT POKER, NO DRAW

Not really a draw game, Straight Poker cannot really be classified elsewhere. In straight draw poker, players make their best five card hand with no wild cards and no draws. There is traditionally only one betting round, and plenty of bluffing in Straight Poker.

Kings and Little Ones

In this popular variation, Kings and the lowest card in each player's hand is wild. A hand of: 10-Q-5-K-Q means the King and the Five are both wild. The pair of queens has just become a Four of a Kind. Because you know that every player at the table has a wild card, remember that hands are going to be big more often than not. If a player is holding an Ace, it is considered High or Low at the player's discretion. An Ace can be used as a Little One.

Honky Tonk

Honky Tonk is a High/Low Draw game where the pot is split between highest and lowest hands. In Honky Tonk, Kings are wild in those hands called Low while Threes are wild in those hands called High.

Jacks or Better, Trips to Win

This game is the most popular qualifier draw game going. Five cards are dealt to each player. The initial betting round can only be opened by a player holding a Pair of Jacks or higher. A player can only win the pot if that player is holding cards that are worth a Three of a Kind or higher. If no player can open the betting round, or if no player can win the game, then each player re-antes and the cards are dealt by the player to the left of the dealer. As was mentioned earlier, **you cannot bluff qualifiers.** The qualifiers must be shown to the table to collect the pot. If a player qualifies with Jacks, but discards one of the pair in a draw, the table can request that they see the Jack in the mucked cards. If no Jack is found, that player has some explaining to do!

PREPARING

BASICS

DRAW

STUD

GUTS

COMMUNITY

HOLD'EM

CASINO

NON-POKER

GLOSSARY

VARIATIONS

One interesting variation to this game comes from Dave Meichsner. Any player who folds throughout any point in the game is out of the game until it's over and somebody has won. If the game is re-dealt because nobody could open with Jacks or nobody could win with Trips, players that folded are not dealt back in on subsequent re-deals. This helps keep people in the game, and keeps the pots healthy.

Jacks and Back

If no player can open with a pair of Jacks or better, then the game is played as Lowball, with one draw and a final betting round. As always, make sure everyone knows what qualifies as the best low hand.

Up and Down the Ladder

Another, less popular version of Jacks or Better states that on the first hand, if no player can open with a pair of Jacks or better, then the game is re-dealt as Queens or Better, Trips to Win. If nobody has Queens or better to open, then this the qualifier becomes Kings or Better, Trips to Win. If no player shows Kings, it moves to Aces or Better. After that, if the game continues, it works back down, from Kings to Queens, to Jacks. This can also be played where players move directly from Aces back down to Jacks or Better.

Jacks or Better, Trips to Win is also commonly played with one qualifier, rather than two. Where players need only the Jacks or better to open or win. If they have Trips, more power to 'em!

43

Trees

Five cards are dealt to each player followed by a betting round.
Players freely exchange cards with other players, always receiving the same number of cards back as they traded away. When all
players are finished trading, there is a final betting round.
The best five card hand wins.

Players are free to trade as
many times as they like, so
long as they always receive
the same number of cards in
return. The trading round
continues until no pair of
players wants to trade any
more cards. When every
player has settled on their
cards, there is a second
betting round followed by a
showdown.

Strategy

The experienced player should
remember which cards have been
given to which players. Players who
are interested in trading three, then
two, then one cards are likely putting
together a straight or flush. Passing
a pair is unwise, as is passing suited
connecting cards to the same player
(Twos, Threes, Fours).

Six Back to Five

Another user-submitted game variation, this one deals each
player six cards. After the first betting round, each player draws
as per normal Draw rules. The exception is that each player
draws one less card than they discard. This means players who
want three new cards must discard four cards out of their hand.

With each player drawing one less card than he or she receives,
all end with five card hand. A final betting round takes place, and
the best five card hand wins the pot.

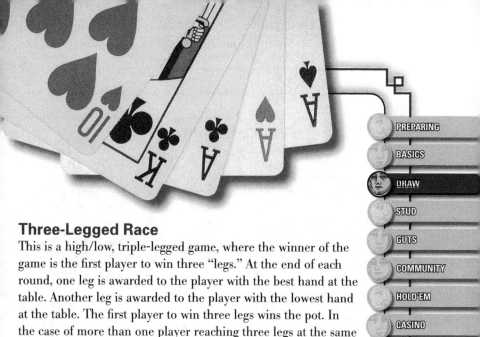

PREPARING

BASICS

DRAW

STUD

GUTS

COMMUNITY

HOLD'EM

CASINO

NON-POKER

GLOSSARY

Three-Legged Race

This is a high/low, triple-legged game, where the winner of the game is the first player to win three "legs." At the end of each round, one leg is awarded to the player with the best hand at the table. Another leg is awarded to the player with the lowest hand at the table. The first player to win three legs wins the pot. In the case of more than one player reaching three legs at the same time, the pot is split.

If dealt as seven card draw, then players have the option of calling "pig." If one such player successfully has both the highest and lowest hand at the table, that player is awarded two legs.

Pass the Trash (Anaconda)

One of the most popular draw games, Pass the Trash or Anaconda starts with seven cards dealt to all players. Players determine which cards they wish to discard. Rather than throwing these cards away as in most Draw games, the cards are passed to the player to the left. From the person's right comes the same amount of cards that the player to the right is discarding. For example, if the dealer determines that there will be one pass of 3 cards, then each player passes the 3 cards they do not want to the left and receives 3 cards from the player to the right; hence, pass the trash. After the cards are passed, players bet and have the showdown with their best five card hand.

VARIATIONS

Pass the Trash is one of the most modified game formats. Here are some of the most common variations of this favorite.

High/Low

The pot is split between the highest hand at the table and the lowest hand at the table. This makes for a more competitive game as players who are dealt rags are still in the hunt to win a piece of the pot.

Passing

The dealer determines how many rounds of passing there will be and how many cards will be passed each round. The popular form is 3 passes, the first is of one card, the second of two cards, and the third of three cards. In this version, the final pass can really damage hands that are already holding a full house or players who are holding low hands and who get passed 3 high cards. Passing is done at the same time, so players cannot look at the cards that have been passed to them until they pass their own cards.

Long time HomePoker.com user Matt Big suggests mixing up the pass so the first is a pass of three cards to your immediate left, followed by a pass of two cards two spots to the left, and a pass of one card three spots to the left. Played as High/Low, things are truly mixed up, with less control over planned exchanges.

VARIATIONS

Roll 'em

Adding this feature to Pass the Trash is almost a requirement, as the passing of cards does not consist of betting rounds and there are no draws to separate betting rounds. Once the passing is completed, "rolling 'em" creates four much-needed betting rounds in this game.

Howdy Doody

This hybrid combines the Honky Tonk High/Low wild card rules with Pass the Trash. The game is played as High/Low Pass the Trash, but Threes are wild in hands that are called High by the player, and Kings are wild in hands that are called Low by the player.

Merry Christmas

Another game sent in by readers. As cards are typically passed to the player to the left, this variation has the pot split between the player with the highest hand and the player sitting to the winner's right. The logic is if the person to your left wins, you're the player that passed those cards and you get half the pot.

PREPARING

BASICS

DRAW

STUD

GUTS

COMMUNITY

HOLD'EM

CASINO

NON-POKER

GLOSSARY

Whiskey Poker

The dealer deals five cards face-down to each player, as well an extra five-card hand, the "kitty." For the first betting round, begin with the player to the dealer's left and continue in a clockwise order around the table. Players have the option of either exchanging their hand with the kitty, or keeping the hand that has been dealt to them. When a player exchanges with the kitty, he or she takes the kitty and turns his or her former hand face-up in the center of the table. If no player decides to exchange with the kitty up to and including the dealer, then the kitty is turned face-up in the center of the table.

Beginning to the left of the player who took the kitty, and continuing in clockwise order around the table, players draw as many cards as they want from the kitty, turning the discards from their own hand face-up in place of the cards taken. This way, each player always has five cards and the kitty always has five cards. This continues around and around the table.

When a player sees fit, that player knocks on the table on his or her turn rather than exchange cards. This signals that each other player will only get one more chance to exchange cards with the kitty. Once the sequence reaches the player to the right of the player who knocked, there is a second and final betting round.

A player may decline from exchanging cards with the kitty, but cannot do so twice in a row. When a player has already declined exchanging cards with the kitty, on that player's next turn, he or she must exchange at least one card or knock.

Italian Poker

Five cards are dealt to each player. The player to the dealer's left opens a betting round. Following the betting round, the dealer deals two cards face-up in the center of the table, placing an indicator of some sort (a coin or chip, for example) on the first card flipped up of the two.

The player to the dealer's left now has the option to draw one or two cards. If the player discards both cards, then the dealer gives the two community cards to that player in exchange. If the player only discards one card, then the dealer gives the card with the indicator on it to the player, puts the indicator on the other card, and flips a new card from the top of the deck to replenish the one that has been given to the player. The same option then goes to the next player in clockwise order. The dealer continues to replenish cards that are taken by players, placing the indicator on the one card that was first flipped of the two. This substitution/draw restricts the draw to one or two cards, and goes right up until the dealer, who has the same option. There is a second betting round, followed by a showdown. The best hand wins the pot.

Frustration (Two Card Draw)

In this variant, only two cards are dealt to each player followed by a betting round. Players are then given an opportunity to draw, followed by a final betting round (unless the dealer specifies more than one draw). Hands consist of either the Pair or a High Card. Suited or connecting cards have no special value.

All For One

Five cards are dealt to each player. After the initial betting round, each player, starting to the left of the dealer, has the option of either drawing **one** card or **all five** cards. After the draw is a second betting round, then, the showdown.

PREPARING

BASICS

DRAW

STUD

GUTS

COMMUNITY

HOLD'EM

CASINO

NON-POKER

GLOSSARY

Psycho

In a sense, this game starts off as five card draw and ends as seven card stud. The dealer should specify a low maximum draw, as the rules will indicate. Five cards are dealt to each player. After a betting round and a draw of cards specified by the dealer before the game, players turn up three cards from their hand. The player with the best hand showing opens up a second betting round.

After the second betting round, each player is dealt another card face up. The player with the best hand showing opens a third betting round.

After the third betting round, each player is dealt a seventh card face down, now having two down, four up, and one down. The player with the best hand showing opens a final betting round, before the showdown.

Assassin

This game is played with a Joker in the deck.

Four cards are dealt face-down on top of a blind card dealt to each player. Players may look at their four-card hands, but are not yet permitted to look at their blind card. A betting round ensues, followed by a draw of up to two cards. A second betting round follows the draw.

After this round of betting, each player flips their blind card face-up for all to see. If a player has the Joker for a blind card, that player has been 'assassinated'; he is out of the game AND must match the amount of money that is in the pot. If a player's blind card is anything other than the Joker, then that card is the fifth card in that player's hand and remains face-up in front of the player.

A third and final betting round follows, after which those remaining players showdown their hands. Best hand wins the pot. If the Joker turns up in a player's hand, then it is considered a wild card.

Pick 'Em Poker

After the ante, each player is dealt two cards. A betting round ensues.

The dealer makes a row of community cards face-up. The number of cards in this row is equal to the number of players in the game **plus one**. With each face-up card, the dealer adds two cards face-down. These face-down cards can be kept beneath, above, or on top of each face-up card, such that there's no mistaking which two face-down cards go with each face-up card.

Beginning with the player to the dealer's left, each player decides which face-up card they want to add to their hand. The player must also take the two face-down cards that come with the face-up card that he has chosen. When it reaches the dealer, the dealer has the choice of one of two face-up cards (and consequent two face-down cards). The three cards that are not chosen by any player are mucked so that no player can see what they were. A betting round ensues.

Beginning to the left of the dealer, each player is allowed a draw of up to two cards from the deck. The final betting round ensues, ending with the showdown.

PREPARING

BASICS

DRAW

STUD

GUTS

COMMUNITY

HOLD'EM

CASINO

NON-POKER

GLOSSARY

The basic concept of Stud Poker games is that each player has a certain number of cards face-down and a certain number face-up. The face-down cards (or cards in the hole) are cards that are visible only to the player holding them. The face-up cards, however, are the ones that all players at the table can see in other players' hands.

A typical seven-card stud game leaves a player with three cards face-down that nobody can see and four cards face-up for the whole table to see. In typical five-card stud, each player has one card face-down and four cards face-up by the end of the game. As is the case in other styles of poker, the variations on these themes are endless.

As per usual, players make the best 5 card hand out of the cards in from of them. If you have three Pairs in a seven-card stud game, you can only make two of them count for your hand.

 **THE FEATURES**

Using Wild Cards in Stud Games

It is rare that the dealer calls a flat-out wild card in most Stud games. A face up wild card would tend to discourage the table from calling a bet. As players are going to have four cards face-up on the table you often see players showing Pairs. A player with an open pair wild would never get a caller. You won't normally hear the dealer declare, "Seven-Card Stud, Kings are wild!"

That would be far too pedestrian for the poker world, the home game needs more flavor, and stipulations are almost always involved. That's not to say that you can't play Seven-Card Stud with Kings wild, but generally cards are only wild if they are face down. You'd be more likely to hear, "Kings are wild in the hole," or "Face-down Kings are wild," from the dealer. Other stipulations could involve a player's lowest card dealt face-down being wild, in which case if a player's lowest card in the hole is a Three, and there is also has a Three among that player's face-up cards, both Threes are wild. Again, it is best when a player's wild cards require that they be face-down. That way, nobody knows who has a wild card in their hand until all is said and done.

PREPARING

BASICS

DRAW

STUD

GUTS

COMMUNITY

HOLD'EM

CASINO

NON-POKER

GLOSSARY

High/Low Stud

This is very common in Stud games. At the end of a High/Low game, the pot is split between the player with the best hand at the table and the player with the worst hand. This is a feature that can be added to just about any Stud game in addition to a game's other rules. It encourages more players to stay in the game longer, although the pot gets split two ways. Players also have the option of calling "pig," that is presenting two different five card hands with their seven cards to attempt to win both High and Low. A player calling "pig" must have both the High and the Low or wins nothing. For example, if a player wins the Low, but not the High, then that player wins nothing and the next best Low hand wins that half of the pot. The player who calls "pig" and wins both wins the entire pot.

Lowball

The lowest hand at the table wins the pot. It sounds simple, but players often have different opinions of what is the best low hand. Be sure that you have a house rule in place to deal with the hierarchy of low hands. The most common form of Lowball sets the A-2-3-4-6 as the best low hand. However, there are many players that do not allow Aces to count as low cards, while other tables play that Straights and Flushes do not count against you. Suffice to say, this can be a real powder keg at showdown if players don't establish a clear rule. Here are some suggestions:

In the most common form of Lowball, Ace can be low, and Straights count against you, A-2-3-4-6 is the best low hand.

When Straights do not count against you and Aces can be low, the perfect low would be A-2-3-4-5.

If Straights do count against you and Aces cannot be low, then you're playing a game called Kansas City Lowball, and the perfect low is 2-3-4-5-7.

New York Stud

This variation, which can be added to any Stud game, stipulates that an outside Straight beats a Pair. An outside Straight is four cards in numerical sequence in a hand, or four cards to a Straight. This stipulation adds a new rank to the *what-beats-what* table. The outside Straight beats a Pair, but loses to Two Pair. If, through the course of the game, a player has the outside straight showing face-up, that player bets over one who only has a Pair showing.

Canadian Stud

This variation plays just like New York Stud, and adds a Fourflush, which beats an outside Straight. A Fourflush is holding four cards of the same suit, or four cards to a flush. This stipulation adds two new ranks to the *what-beats-what* table. The outside Straight beats a Pair, the Fourflush beats an outside straight, but Two Pair beats a Fourflush. A player with a Fourflush showing bets over a player with an outside Straight showing, who bets over a player with a Pair showing. Note that holding four cards to a

Straight Flush is no better than a Fourflush. In fact, it is nothing more than a Fourflush.

PREPARING

BASICS

DRAW

STUD

GUTS

COMMUNITY

HOLD'EM

CASINO

NON-POKER

GLOSSARY

Spanish Stud

To play Spanish Stud, all Twos, Threes, Fours, Fives, and Sixes are removed from the deck. This is a total of 20 cards removed, leaving 32 cards that are played. Spanish Five-Card Stud could be played at six people, but Spanish Seven-Card stud could be played by a maximum of four players if only one deck is used.

Bet or Drop

The stipulation added here is that the player who opens the betting round does so by having the best hand showing. This player must open with at least the table's minimum bet or fold. The option to check or pass is removed. Typically, the dealer announces a slight increase in the table's minimum bet for the purposes of this variation.

Cold Hands (Showdown)

This is a less popular variation where the ante is significantly higher, but there are no betting rounds. All cards are dealt face-up in sequence and the best hand wins. Typically on top of winning a set pot, a Cold Hand is used to determine the first dealer of the night, or as a final quick game.

MODIFIED WHAT BEATS WHAT NEW YORK AND CANADIAN STUD
THREE-OF-A-KIND
TWO PAIR
FOURFLUSH (CANADIAN STUD)
OUTSIDE STRAIGHT (NEW YORK & CANADIAN STUD)
PAIR
HIGH CARD

Basic Five-Card Stud

One card is dealt face-down to each player, followed by one card face-up to each player. A betting round ensues, opened by the player with the highest card showing. Another card is dealt face-up to each player, followed by another betting round, opened by the player with the best hand showing. This continues until each player has one card face-down, four cards face-up, and there have been four betting rounds. The best hand wins the pot.

Five-Card Stud is typically dealt one card down, four up. This format can be changed to two down, three up (making three betting rounds), or three down, two up (making two betting rounds). Another popular variation is to deal the first card face-down, the next three cards face-up, and the fifth card face-down.

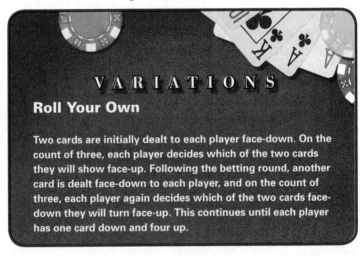

VARIATIONS

Roll Your Own

Two cards are initially dealt to each player face-down. On the count of three, each player decides which of the two cards they will show face-up. Following the betting round, another card is dealt face-down to each player, and on the count of three, each player again decides which of the two cards face-down they will turn face-up. This continues until each player has one card down and four up.

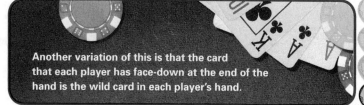

PREPARING

BASICS

DRAW

STUD

GUTS

COMMUNITY

HOLD'EM

CASINO

NON-POKER

GLOSSARY

Another variation of this is that the card that each player has face-down at the end of the hand is the wild card in each player's hand.

Basic Seven Card Stud

The dealer begins by dealing two cards face down to each player, and one card dealt face up to each player. The player with the highest card showing opens the first betting round. Following this betting round, another card is dealt face-up to each player, followed by a betting round, followed by a third card face-up, followed by a betting round, followed by a fourth card face-up, followed by a betting round, followed by the last card dealt face-down, concluded by the final betting round.

The player that opens each betting round is the player that has the best hand showing out of the cards face-up. If, for example, every player is dealt face-up mismatched cards, except for one player who has a pair showing, then that player opens the betting round.

In the end, each player takes the five cards out of seven that make up the best hand. For example, if a player is dealt the following hand:

The best combination of five cards in this player's hand are the 3 Kings and the pair of Twos. This player has a Full House, Kings over Twos.

VARIATIONS

Kankakee

Played as regular Seven-Card Stud except that the first card dealt face up to each player, after each player already has two cards dealt face down, and all matching cards, are wild in that player's hand.

Six-Card Stud

Six cards are dealt to each player in a combination of some up and some in the hole. Popular versions are one down, five up or one down, four up, one down or two down, four up. Players make their best five card hand with the six cards.

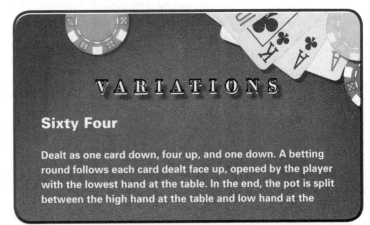

VARIATIONS

Sixty Four

Dealt as one card down, four up, and one down. A betting round follows each card dealt face up, opened by the player with the lowest hand at the table. In the end, the pot is split between the high hand at the table and low hand at the

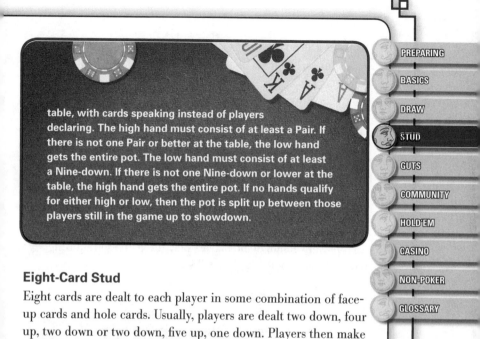

table, with cards speaking instead of players declaring. The high hand must consist of at least a Pair. If there is not one Pair or better at the table, the low hand gets the entire pot. The low hand must consist of at least a Nine-down. If there is not one Nine-down or lower at the table, the high hand gets the entire pot. If no hands qualify for either high or low, then the pot is split up between those players still in the game up to showdown.

PREPARING

BASICS

DRAW

STUD

GUTS

COMMUNITY

HOLD'EM

CASINO

NON-POKER

GLOSSARY

Eight-Card Stud

Eight cards are dealt to each player in some combination of face-up cards and hole cards. Usually, players are dealt two down, four up, two down or two down, five up, one down. Players then make their best five card hand with the eight cards.

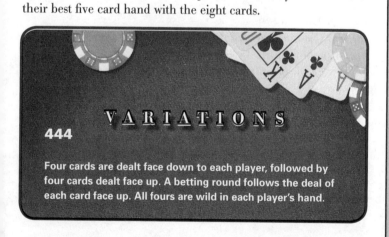

VARIATIONS

444

Four cards are dealt face down to each player, followed by four cards dealt face up. A betting round follows the deal of each card face up. All fours are wild in each player's hand.

Sevens Take All

This stud variation makes a pair of Sevens the best hand a player can get.

Suspense is generated when a player is dealt a Seven face up. The table doesn't know if that player has the other Seven underneath. Even if the player doesn't, they can still play a strong bluff. Nothing beats Sevens, except a player who also has a Pair of Sevens and higher kicker.

Kings and Little Ones

Kings are always wild, as well as the lowest face-down card in each player's hand. Some players play this game so that King must also be face down to be wild.

Litte Ones (Low Hole)

The lowest card dealt face down to each player is wild in that player's hand. This game is otherwise known as Low Hole.

Follow the Queen

Standard Seven-Card Stud with Queens wild. Throughout the course of the deal, if a Queen is dealt face-up to a player, then the card that is face-up after that Queen is called the trailer and it also becomes wild. These Queens and trailers are also wild in determining who has the best hand showing to open each betting round.

If during the course of the game another Queen is dealt face-up to a player, then the trailer that follows the usurping Queen is now the new wild card along with the Queens. The old trailer is no longer wild, so you never have more than Queens and one other card wild. Queens and cards matching the current trailer are also wild if they are dealt face-down. As usual, the best five card hand wins.

If no Queen shows up at all, no cards are wild.

PREPARING

BASICS

DRAW

STUD

GUTS

COMMUNITY

HOLD'EM

CASINO

NON-POKER

GLOSSARY

VARIATIONS

Follow the Cowboy

Played the same as Follow the Queen, except it is the card that follows a King that is wild, instead of a Queen.

Next in the John

Played the same as Follow the Queen, except that trailers follow Jacks instead of Queens.

Good Tithings

Players who are dealt face up Queens are forced to pay a small amount to stay in the game. Players who are showing a trailer face up also pay a small tax to stay in the hand. Usually these amounts are small. For example, 50 cents for the Queen, 25 cents for the trailer.

Some players play that if no Queen has been dealt face-up after every player has been dealt their four face-up cards, then players must re-ante and the game is re-dealt until a Queen appears face up. Note that the final down cards are not dealt in this variant.

Roll Your Own (Mexican Stud)

The theme of this game is that each player chooses which of their cards they will show to the rest of the table, while maintaining the format of three cards face-down and four face-up. Each player is dealt three cards face-down. On the count of three, each player chooses which of the three to turn face-up to the rest of the table. This is followed by a betting round, opened by the player with the highest card showing. Another card is dealt face-down to each player, and each player again must turn one of them face-up on the count of three. This continues until each player has been dealt a total of six cards and there have been four betting rounds. At this point, each player has two cards face-down and four cards face-up. The seventh and final card is dealt face-down, and the final betting round is opened by the player with the best hand showing. The player who makes the best five card hand takes the pot.

Strategies

The purpose of players choosing which cards to show the table is set up their betting strategy. Players with bad hands can show the table their best cards to try to intimidate. For the opposite effect, players with good hands can show only their weak and mismatched cards to the rest of the table to give the impression of a weaker hand. This also allows a player to make a decision about driving the betting. A player showing high cards opens any betting round, which can be turned to an advantage with a strong hand.

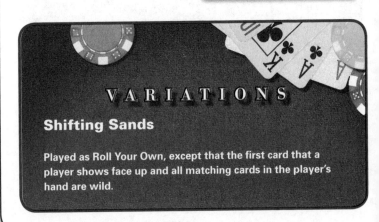

VARIATIONS

Shifting Sands

Played as Roll Your Own, except that the first card that a player shows face up and all matching cards in the player's hand are wild.

PREPARING

BASICS

DRAW

STUD

GUTS

COMMUNITY

HOLD'EM

CASINO

NON-POKER

GLOSSARY

Monterey

Played as Roll Your Own, except that each player's final hole card and all matching cards are wild. A player's wild card isn't determined until the end of the game with this twist, so anything can happen here.

Flip

Four cards are dealt face down to each player. Each player flips face up any two cards of their choice, followed by a betting round opened by the player with the best hand showing. Regular Seven-Card Stud ensues with two more cards dealt face up and the final card dealt face down. The best hand claims the pot.

Murder

This is played like typical Seven-Card Stud with two cards down, four up, then the final card down. Betting rounds work as in normal Stud, except with one stipulation. If a player is dealt a card face-up that matches a card that player already has face-up, meaning if a player has a Pair showing, then that player either folds or matches the amount of money in the pot to stay in the game. If a player has two matching cards (Three-of-a-Kind), that player can fold or pay double the pot. Other than this stipulation, the game is dealt and hands are counted as normal Seven-Card Stud.

It stands to reason that the best and cheapest hand to hold is a flush or a straight, a good hand with no matching cards.

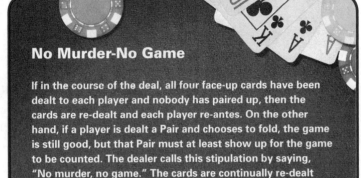

No Murder-No Game

If in the course of the deal, all four face-up cards have been dealt to each player and nobody has paired up, then the cards are re-dealt and each player re-antes. On the other hand, if a player is dealt a Pair and chooses to fold, the game is still good, but that Pair must at least show up for the game to be counted. The dealer calls this stipulation by saying, "No murder, no game." The cards are continually re-dealt until a pair has shown in the course of a game.

Homicide

This variation is played where seven cards are still dealt, but one card is dealt face-down, followed by six cards face up. The odds are far more likely that somebody if not several people are going to match up, not to mention that there would be six betting rounds altogether. Players are helped through this torment of a game by the fact that if a player's down card matches any card that has been dealt to him face-up, those cards are wild. For example, if a player's card in the hole is a Three and another Three is dealt face-up to that player, both of those Threes are wild. If a player's card in the hole matches no card that the player has face-up, then no cards in that player's hand are wild. This is an expensive game.

High Chicago

The player with the best hand gets half of the pot. The other half of the pot goes to the player who has the highest Spade card face-down. If a player has the King of Spades, but it was dealt to that player face-up, that does not count; it must have been dealt face-down. The Ace of Spades is obviously the nut Spade unless previously dealt face-up, and any player who is dealt the Ace face-down knows that they automatically receive half the pot.

When the game ends, it might end up being the Six of Spades that is the highest Spade dealt face-down, for example, and that player would get half the pot for it.

PREPARING

BASICS

DRAW

STUD

GUTS

COMMUNITY

HOLD'EM

CASINO

NON-POKER

GLOSSARY

VARIATIONS

Some people play this game where players must call their hands either "best hand" or "high Spade" before everybody shows their hand. By calling your hand, you are indicating which of the two you are going for. In other words, if you call "best hand" but end up having the highest Spade face-down, you do not get half of the pot for that Spade, because "high Spade" is not what you were going for. After everybody has called their hand, those who called "best hand" compare hands to determine who wins half of the pot among them, while the players who called "high Spade" compare their highest Spade card face-down for the other half of the pot.

Low Chicago

The exact same rules apply except in this game, the pot is split between the player with the best hand and the player who has the lowest Spade card face-down. The dealer who calls this game needs to specify whether or not the Ace of Spades will be counted as the lowest Spade card, or whether it is the Two of Spades. This is a discrepancy because the Ace is typically considered the highest card of the suit, but nevertheless, it can be used to make a straight from Ace to Five and is therefore, a low card. This should be determined before the hand is dealt.

Black Mariah

This term is used to describe a hand that is not only the best hand at the table but is also the hand that was dealt the highest Spade card face-down. That player would thus win the entire pot. When the game Black Mariah is called, it is a game that only ends when a single player has the best hand at the table and is dealt the highest Spade card face-down. If the best hand and highest Spade are in two different hands, then everybody re-antes, and the game is re-dealt by the player to the left of the dealer, and replayed. This continues until a single player has the best hand and highest Spade face-down. One of the only ways to end this game is by continually betting the maximum bet after being dealt the Ace of Spades (or a high enough Spade), bluffing the other players out of the hand. You may not have the best hand at the table, but players who do not continue to see bets are out of the game. When only one player is left in the game, the game is obviously over, assuming that one player has at least one Spade card face-down.

Blind Baseball (No-Peek Baseball)

Seven cards are all immediately dealt face-down. Players keep their seven cards face-down without looking at them. The first player to the left of the dealer flips over his or her first card. Based on that card, he or she opens a betting round. That face-up card is now the best hand showing at the table. After the betting round, the next player flips over cards until his or her cards face-up beat the best hand showing. For example, if the first player turned up a Jack, then the next player flips over cards until what is showing beats a Jack high card. Those cards showing now become the new best hand at the table, and that player opens a betting round. This continues with each player flipping over cards until they can beat the best hand showing at the table, opening a betting round after they have done so.

There are two ways that players are removed from this game. If a player has flipped over all of his or her cards and cannot beat the best hand at the table with what is showing, then that player is out of the game. Players that do not at least see each bet that comes their way are out of the game. The game ends when all players have flipped over all of their cards. The best hand wins.

Baseball

Blind Baseball is not basic Baseball, only the more popular version. Basic Baseball (or just Baseball) is a standard Seven-Card Stud game, in which Threes and Nines are wild, and a Four dealt face-up allows you to receive a new card from the deck. These Threes, Fours, and Nines typically cost a player a predetermined

PREPARING

BASICS

DRAW

STUD

GUTS

COMMUNITY

HOLD'EM

CASINO

NON-POKER

GLOSSARY

fee in order to take advantage of them. At a quarter-table, for example, it may be a quarter for a Three or Nine to be counted as wild, and 2 quarters to get an extra card from the Four.

VARIATIONS

Most people think that there should be special cards in this game that revolve around a baseball theme. For example:

Innings

Nine cards dealt instead of seven, called "nine innings".

Wild cards

Threes and Nines are wild, modeled after three strikes, three outs, nine innings, and nine players. Other people play that when players turn up a card that is wild, they must pay for that card to be wild, usually a small amount like a quarter at a nickel-ante table.

Extra Card

If a player flips up a Four, modeled after four balls and four bases, that player is dealt an extra card face-down from the deck. Other people play that if a player flips up a Four and wants the extra card, it must be paid for, typically 50 cents at a nickel-ante table. Other than that, the card does not contribute anything to the hand other than being a regular Four. However, getting the extra card can really help a hand.

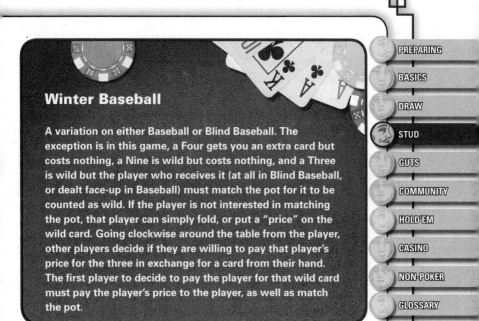

Winter Baseball

A variation on either Baseball or Blind Baseball. The exception is in this game, a Four gets you an extra card but costs nothing, a Nine is wild but costs nothing, and a Three is wild but the player who receives it (at all in Blind Baseball, or dealt face-up in Baseball) must match the pot for it to be counted as wild. If the player is not interested in matching the pot, that player can simply fold, or put a "price" on the wild card. Going clockwise around the table from the player, other players decide if they are willing to pay that player's price for the three in exchange for a card from their hand. The first player to decide to pay the player for that wild card must pay the player's price to the player, as well as match the pot.

PREPARING

BASICS

DRAW

STUD

GUTS

COMMUNITY

HOLD'EM

CASINO

NON-POKER

GLOSSARY

The Queen

In this Stud variation, if the Queen of Spades is dealt face-up to any player at any point in the game, all of the cards are collected by the player to the dealer's left. All players re-ante into what has amassed in the pot so far and the hand is re-dealt from scratch. The game is reset but now, there is all of the money that has collected from the previous round of play. Also, if the Queen of Spades is dealt face-down to any player, then it is wild in that player's hand, revealed at the end of the game. If the Queen of Spades is not dealt at all throughout the course of game, then it is played as standard Seven-Card Stud with no cards wild and no stipulations.

For some reason, the Queen of Spades is the focal point of many Stud games. According to historians, the division of playing cards into suits and symbols takes place in Europe in the 15th century. The French were the first to identify the characters in court cards. The Queen of Spades was to be a representation of Pallas Athene, the Greek goddess of Wisdom and War, and the only armed queen in the deck.

Auction

The dealer deals two face-down cards to each player. A betting round is opened by the player sitting to the left of the dealer. A number of cards equal to the number of players are then flipped face-up onto the table. Each player chooses one of these cards to go face-up into their hand. To determine which player gets which card, each player including the dealer, chooses a sum of money ranging from the table's minimum bet to the table's maximum bet, hiding this money in their hands. At the same time, each player drops the money they are holding in their hand. The player who drops the highest sum of money gets the first pick of the face-up community cards. The player who drops the second highest sum of money gets second pick of the community cards, and so on. If two players drop the same amount of money, the one sitting closest to the dealer in clockwise sequence picks first. By the end of this auction round, each player has the original two cards dealt to them face-down as well as one card face-up. The dealer then flips another set of community cards, equal in number to the number of players at the table, and another auction round ensues.

There are four auction rounds in total, after which each player will have their two original face-down cards, and four cards face-up, the ones that each player chose on the auction rounds.

A betting round ensues. The seventh and final card is dealt face-down to each player, followed by the third and final betting round. The best hand wins the pot.

Because of the four auction rounds, play in this game can be slow. Players are normally reminded at the game's beginning that it's going to be a long game, and that the auction rounds should go as quickly as possible. At a nickel-table with betting numbers ranging from 5 cents to 25 or 50 cents, the amount of money a player chooses to auction can vary greatly and be factored into a player's auctioning strategy. At a quarter-table however, where bets vary less (usually being either one quarter or two quarters), the dealer needs to decide if players can bid more money than the table's usual maximum bet. The dealer at a quarter-table that has a fifty-cent maximum bet may determine that players can bid up to a dollar on auction rounds.

PREPARING

BASICS

DRAW

STUD

GUTS

COMMUNITY

HOLD'EM

CASINO

NON-POKER

GLOSSARY

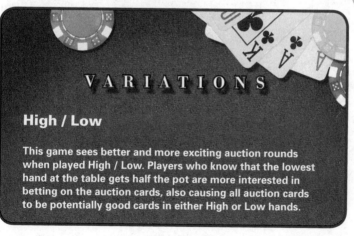

VARIATIONS

High / Low

This game sees better and more exciting auction rounds when played High / Low. Players who know that the lowest hand at the table gets half the pot are more interested in betting on the auction cards, also causing all auction cards to be potentially good cards in either High or Low hands.

Betting Rounds

Some masochists enjoy a betting round after each auction round. This would eliminate the first betting round that follows the initial deal of two face-down cards. The first betting round then follows the first auction round, as well as a betting round after each auction round, then the final betting round following the deal of the seventh card face-down to each player. The problem with this variation is that players need an extra reminder on how quickly play needs to go. Otherwise, a game consisting of four auction rounds and five betting rounds makes for an extremely long game. Think about the length of a normal Seven-Card Stud game, then add the time difference of a dealer simply dealing face-up cards to each player and that of players going through a lengthy auction round each time.

Five Card Stud

The game can also be played with a Five-Card Stud format. One card is dealt face-down to each player, followed by a betting round, followed by four auction rounds, followed by a final betting round. Playing a seven card version provides an extra betting round and more opportunity in a game like this with its two extra face-down cards.

Count Your Diamonds

This is played as regular Five or Seven-Card Stud. The pot gets split in half, with one half going to the player with the best poker hand. After this, each player adds the numbers on all of the Diamond-suited cards in their hand, whether dealt face-up or face-down. Two to Ten counts as the number, the Ace of Diamonds counts as fourteen, the Jack counts as eleven, the

Queen counts as twelve, and the King counts as thirteen. All the Diamonds in a player's hand are tallied together as a point score. The player with the highest number of 'Diamonds points' gets the other half of the pot.

Countdown

This game has a wild card, determined only after all of the cards have been dealt. After the betting round that follows the deal of the seventh and final card, the number of players remaining in the game becomes the card number that is wild. If, for example, five players start this game, and after the last betting round of the game, only three players remain, then Threes are wild in everybody's hand.

Considering most poker games consist of a table of five to seven players, it's safe to assume in this one that only a low card is going to end up being wild. What is more, the challenge is trying to bet strategically as to plan the number of people that remain in the game.

Echo Park

This is a variant of Five-Card stud, but before dealing a second card to each player, players decide if they wish to receive that card face-up or face-down. If the player chooses to receive the card face-up, then the dealer flips a card face-up to that player as normal. If the player chooses to receive the card face-down, then that player signals so by flipping the current hole card face-up. The dealer gives the same option to every player around the table. Now, each player has one card in the hole and one face-up. The highest card face-up opens the first betting round.

The dealer begins dealing a third card to each player. If the player wants the third card face-up, the dealer deals it face-up. If the player wants the third card face-down, then that player

PREPARING

BASICS

DRAW

STUD

GUTS

COMMUNITY

HOLD'EM

CASINO

NON-POKER

GLOSSARY

signals
by flipping
up the current
hole card.
Another betting
round ensues.

The same is done with the
fourth and fifth cards to each player
so that at all times up until the end of the
game, each player has one card in the hole
and the rest face-up.

VARIATIONS

Wild in the Hole

A good variation to this game is that the player's hole card
at the end of the game is wild. This has more of an effect on
what card each player keeps in the hole. If, for example, a
player has a Queen in the hole at the game's end and another
Queen face-up, then both are wild.

High / Low

Michael, who sent this game, suggests playing it as High /
Low, which is a good idea if your table is not big on All-High
Five-Card Stud.

The Deck

The dealer deals a card face-down to each player, then exposes the top card of the deck. The first player to the left of the dealer has the option of either choosing the exposed card or a blind one from the top of the deck. Whichever choice the player makes, that card is dealt face-up. If a player chooses the exposed card, then the dealer replaces it with the next card off the top of the deck and gives the same choice to the next player. If that player chose a blind card, then the next player is given the option to take the exposed card or a blind one. The exposed card is not replaced until it is either chosen by a player or the dealer turns it down. Once the dealer turns it down, the round of dealing is over, followed by a betting round.

When the next round of dealing starts after the betting round, whichever card was exposed is placed at the bottom of the deck, replaced by a new card from the top of the deck. This continues until each player has one card in the hole and four cards face-up. There is a final betting round and the best hand wins.

PREPARING

BASICS

DRAW

STUD

GUTS

COMMUNITY

HOLD'EM

CASINO

NON-POKER

GLOSSARY

BLIND

This is not a true Stud game, but is too difficult to categorize anywhere else.

It's played with seven cards or, more commonly, with five cards. All cards are dealt face-down as in Draw Poker, but all cards are dealt one at a time, as in Stud Poker. All betting rounds are opened by the player to the dealer's left. The dealer deals one card face-down to each player, followed by a betting round, followed by a second card to each player, followed by a betting round, and so on.

If a betting round ensues after each card dealt, then there will be five betting rounds with five cards, and seven betting rounds with seven cards. The dealer who calls this game may choose to only start the betting after each player has been dealt 2-3 cards, especially with seven cards.

Three-Card Monte

See also **Monte Carlo** in the Guts Poker section.

Cards are dealt one face-down to each player, followed by two face-up to each player. The dealer determines beforehand if there is a betting round preceding the first card dealt face-up, but at the very least, one betting round ensues after each of the two face-up cards are dealt.

There are a number of ways to determine what hand beats what hand in Three-Card Monte, but the following are three common examples:

Version #1
(based only on possible poker hands witah three cards)

- High Card
- Pair
- Three-of-a kind

Version #2
(based on the conventional rank of poker hands, with the exception of the Straight Flush)

- High Card
- Pair
- Three-card Straight
- Three-card Flush
- Three-card Straight Flush
- Three-of-a-Kind

Version #3
(based on the actual odds of being dealt each hand)

- High Card
- Pair
- Three-card Flush
- Three-card Straight
- Three-of-a-Kind
- Three-card Straight Flush

Take It or Leave It

Played as Five-Card Stud poker. The dealer deals one card face down to each player. The dealer then deals a second card face down to the player to his or her left. That player has the option of keeping that card or passing it to the next player. If that player keeps it, he or she flips it face up. If that player passes it, he or she is dealt their second card face up (in other words, turning down the first card means you are automatically stuck with the second card). The next player either has the card passed by the first player or is dealt one face down from the dealer. That player has the same option to keep or pass. This continues around the table up to the dealer.

With each player having one card down and one up, the player with the best hand (highest card) showing opens a betting round. Following the betting round, the dealer again deals a card face down to the first player, who can keep or pass.

This continues until each player has one card face down and four face up, followed by a final betting round. The best hand wins the pot.

PREPARING

BASICS

DRAW

STUD

GUTS

COMMUNITY

HOLD'EM

CASINO

NON-POKER

GLOSSARY

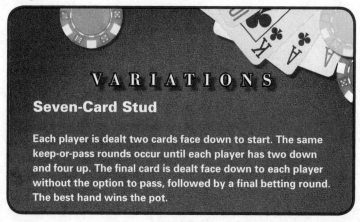

VARIATIONS

Seven-Card Stud

Each player is dealt two cards face down to start. The same keep-or-pass rounds occur until each player has two down and four up. The final card is dealt face down to each player without the option to pass, followed by a final betting round. The best hand wins the pot.

Pig

Each player is dealt three cards face down, followed by a betting round opened by the player to the dealer's left.

Each player is then dealt one card face up, followed by a betting round opened by the player with the highest card showing. A second card is dealt face up, followed by another betting round, opened by the player with the best hand showing.

Players then take their two face up cards and turn them face down, picking up their five cards in their hand. A draw round follows, where players may discard from their hand and draw new cards from the deck. Having turned their cards face down, players do not know what cards each other player is discarding. There is a final betting round, and the best hand wins.

Hurricane

This is Two-Card Stud poker. One card is dealt face-down, followed by a betting round, followed by one card dealt face-up, followed by a second betting round opened by the player with the highest card showing. Hands consist either of a Pair or a High Card.

Obviously, this game is one that may require some 'spice' in order to be enjoyable. Suggestions include playing High/Low, or even including a draw of one card and an additional betting round after the second betting round.

English Stud Poker

This is dealt as standard Seven-Card Stud with two down, four up, and one down. The first two cards down and third card up are dealt, followed by a betting round. The fourth card is dealt face-up, followed by a betting round. The fifth card is dealt face-up, followed by a draw in which players have the option to discard one card from their hand for a new one from the deck. If the player discards one that was face-down, that player receives the new card face-down. If the player discards one that was face-up, that player receives the new card face-up. The draw is followed by a betting round.

A sixth card is dealt face-up, followed by another draw of one card, and another betting round. The seventh card is dealt face-down, followed by a final draw of one card, followed by the final betting round.

PREPARING

BASICS

DRAW

STUD

GUTS

COMMUNITY

HOLD'EM

CASINO

NON-POKER

GLOSSARY

Second Hand High

In Seven-Card Stud poker, the pot is won by the player who has the second best hand at the table at showdown. If only one player remains in the game, that player wins by default.

Sequence

In Seven-Card Stud, if throughout the course of cards being dealt face-up, a Two appears, then all Twos are wild in all hands. If this is established, and later a Three appears, then all Threes are wild in all hands with Twos no longer wild. These cards must appear in sequence, and this wild-card reversal continues to Fours and up, should they be dealt face-up in the game. If a Two does not appear throughout the course of the game, then there is nothing wild, and it is played as regular Seven-Card Stud.

Have A Heart

In Seven-Card Stud, if throughout the course of cards being dealt face-up, a player is dealt any Heart, then that player has the option to take any face-up card from any player at the table.

The player with the Heart does not need to discard a card from his or her hand, nor does the player whose card has been taken get a replacement. The player with the Heart takes the new card face-up in his or her hand. This occurs with each Heart dealt face-up throughout the course of the game.

Dirty Schultz
In Seven-Card Stud, if throughout the course of cards being dealt face-up, a player makes a Pair, then the next card dealt face-up and all matching cards are wild.

If, later in the same hand, a player pairs up again, then the next card dealt up is wild, with the old wild card no longer wild.

The Good, The Bad, and The Ugly
This is Seven-Card Stud with three cards dealt face-down in the center of the table. The game proceeds as regular Seven-Card Stud.

Following the second betting round, after each player has been dealt four cards, two up, two down, the dealer flips the first table card (The Good). Any cards in any hand matching The Good are wild, although the card itself is not a community card.

Following the third betting round, after each player has five cards, the dealer flips the second table card (The Bad). Any cards in any player's hand, up or down, matching The Bad must be discarded.

Following the fourth betting round, after each player has six cards, the dealer flips the third table card (The Ugly). Any player who has a card face-up that matching The Ugly is automatically out of the game. Remaining players proceed with the seventh card and final betting round, followed by showdown.

Spots

This is Seven-Card Stud dealt two down, four up, one down. The lowest card dealt face-down to each player is wild in that player's hand.

At showdown, the pot is split between the best hand at the table and the hand containing the highest number of spots. Spots refers to the number of suit symbols in the center column of each card. For example, a Three has three spots, an Ace has one spot, an Eight has two spots.

In case you do not follow how spots are counted, it goes as follows: Ace 1, Two 2, Three 3, Four 0, Five 1, Six 0, Seven 1, Eight 2, Nine 1, Ten 2, Face 0.

PREPARING

BASICS

DRAW

STUD

GUTS

COMMUNITY

HOLD'EM

CASINO

NON-POKER

GLOSSARY

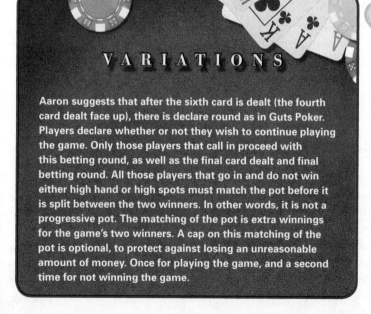

VARIATIONS

Aaron suggests that after the sixth card is dealt (the fourth card dealt face up), there is declare round as in Guts Poker. Players declare whether or not they wish to continue playing the game. Only those players that call in proceed with this betting round, as well as the final card dealt and final betting round. All those players that go in and do not win either high hand or high spots must match the pot before it is split between the two winners. In other words, it is not a progressive pot. The matching of the pot is extra winnings for the game's two winners. A cap on this matching of the pot is optional, to protect against losing an unreasonable amount of money. Once for playing the game, and a second time for not winning the game.

High/Low Jim

Seven cards are immediately dealt face down to each player. This is a High/Low game where players make their best, or worst, five card hand. Of the two kickers left over, players leave one to the side, but keep the other in their hand. Players put their six cards on the table with a pile of four cards in the middle and a single card on each side of the pile.

Simultaneously, players flip over one card at a time from their four-card pile. A betting round ensues each flip, opened by the player with the best hand showing.

After the fourth betting round (when each player should have their entire four-card pile flipped over, leaving only the two single cards), players simultaneously flip over either the left card or the right card. A player who flips over his or her left card is signaling going low. A player who flips over his or her right card is signaling going high. In other words, the card not flipped over is the second kicker that was kept from the beginning of the hand. Winners of the High and Low hands split the pot.

Breed the Heifer

This is Seven-Card Stud dealt two down, four up, one down or in whichever format works best for you.

When a player is dealt a card face-up that matches any card the player has already been dealt face-up, then the next card dealt from the deck is wild in all players' hands. For example, Player #1 has a Two and a Five showing. Player #1 is dealt another Two face-up and the next card dealt to Player #2 is a Jack. Jacks are now wild in every players' hand.

When another player pairs up later in the game, the card that was the wild card is replaced by the next card dealt face-up. The old wild card is no longer wild. If the final card dealt face-up pairs up for that player, then there is no wild card, as there are no more cards to be dealt face-up.

PREPARING

BASICS

DRAW

STUD

GUTS

COMMUNITY

HOLD'EM

CASINO

NON-POKER

GLOSSARY

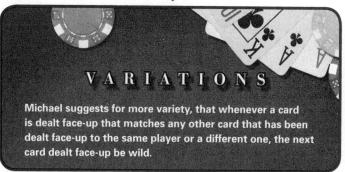

V A R I A T I O N S

Michael suggests for more variety, that whenever a card is dealt face-up that matches any other card that has been dealt face-up to the same player or a different one, the next card dealt face-up be wild.

Bid 'Em

There are a number of values that the dealer needs to determine prior to dealing this game. In the explanation that follows, example values have been given, but they need to be tailored, based on your table stakes.

One card is dealt face-down to each player. The dealer then flips the top card of the deck face-up next to the deck. The player to the dealer's left is given the first option of either bidding 25 cents on the visible card or paying 50 cents for a blind card from the deck. If the player takes a blind card, then it is dealt face-up in that player's hand, and the same option is presented to the next player, using the same visible card.

If the player bids on the visible card, then any other player following in sequence, and who has not yet received a card, has the option of bidding more for that card than the opening 25 cents. The player who bids the most puts that amount of money into the pot and gets the card. A new card is flipped from the top of the deck to replace it. The option to bid on the visible card or pay for a blind card continues around the table until each player receives another card. Players who received a card out of sequence by outbidding the rest of the table are skipped over until every player has received one new card.

After every player has a new card, the visible card is discarded. A betting round follows, opened by the player with the highest card showing. A new card is flipped over from the top of the deck, and another bid/buy round ensues. This time, it is the player two seats to the left of the dealer that bids first. Each bid/buy round is followed by a betting round.

Once each player has four cards—the initial buried card, and three new cards from bid/buy rounds—each is dealt a free card face-down from the top of the deck. After another betting round, players are given the option to exchange one card from their

hand for a new card from the deck for $1. If they are discarding a down card, they receive the new one down. If discarding an up card, they receive the new one up. After a final betting round, the best hand wins.

PREPARING

BASICS

DRAW

STUD

GUTS

COMMUNITY

HOLD'EM

CASINO

NON-POKER

GLOSSARY

VARIATIONS

High/Low

Michael suggests that this game be played High/Low.

Super Bid 'Em

This is played the same as Bid 'Em, with one exception. Instead of players only being able to bid if they have not received a card that round, players may bid as many times as they want in a round, up to a maximum of three bid cards. After three bid cards, they participate in betting rounds, but wait until all other players have a total of four cards, which precedes the free card that is dealt to each player. When determining who gets the chance to bid first, it follows regular Bid 'Em rules, but if a player has more bid cards than there have been bid rounds, then it is the next player who bids first.

GUTS
POKER

To qualify as Guts poker, a game must include a round after the cards are dealt where players decide if they are in or out of the game. Those players that call out have no further stakes in the hand. Those players that called in continue playing. Of those players who called in, the one who has the best hand collects the pot. All other players who called in and did not have the best hand at the table must match the amount of money in the pot. Now, there is an equal or greater amount of money in the pot, even after the round has ended. So, the cards are picked up, shuffled, and the same game is dealt again, with players again deciding if they will go in or out. This continues until only one player goes in, then that player wins the pot and the game is over. Doing the math, if three people call "in", the amount of money in the pot doubles. One person wins the money, while the other two match the pot. Guts games are characterized by this calling of in or out as well as the growing size of the pot The game being played continues until only one person calls in and wins. Note that, for this reason, Guts games are typically more expensive to play. While pots grow in Guts poker, so does the excitement. Mixing up your regular night with some Guts can help keep things interesting. That said, Guts poker can also get out of control if players start chasing after some bad beats. For this reason, caps are used.

THE FEATURES

PREPARING

BASICS

DRAW

STUD

GUTS

COMMUNITY

HOLD'EM

CASINO

NON-POKER

GLOSSARY

Caps

Guts games are where the term "small stakes" is thrown out the window. People often assume that $10 - $30 should suffice for a night of playing Home poker, but a good game of Jacks and Piss may see the pot rise higher than a week's pay. For this reason, some people play with caps. Caps limit how big the pot can get and how much money a player can lose in one hand.

For example, the dealer who calls the Guts game may determine that there is a $5 cap on the game. What this means is that if the pot ever reaches more than five dollars, a player who wins it only claims five dollars of it, and a player who loses only pays five dollars. A cap means that no player can win or lose more than that amount of money. If, for example, there are six dollars in the pot and three players go in, the one of the three who wins, who would normally collect all six dollars, collects only five of the six dollars in the pot. The two of the three who lose, who would normally pay all six dollars, pay only five dollars into the pot.

The advantage to this is that players do not lose their shirts, they only lose as much as the cap. The first disadvantage to this is that a lone player who goes in on a six dollar pot only claims five of it, and the game is re-dealt for the new one dollar pot (which goes against the Guts principle that when a single player goes in, the game is over). This leads into the second disadvantage, which is that the game is played much longer because a $10 pot, for example, requires at least two wins to clear it out, even if a single player goes in each time. The third disadvantage is that caps are supposed to be to players' benefit, whereas it normally encourages them to call in more, knowing they can lose no more than the pot's cap. If a pot exceeds players' expectations, it is because of bad calls and bad luck, two things that are supposed to contribute to a bigger pot in Guts games.

The Kitty

This is a blind hand dealt face-down and not revealed to the table until the hand is over. If the particular Guts games involves five cards being dealt to each player, then a five-card kitty is dealt as well, kept near the dealer, and only turned up at the end of the round. The purpose of the kitty is that those players who go in must not only beat the other players who have gone in but they must also beat the kitty's hand. It is the extra hand that belongs to the pot that nobody sees until the end of the round. The feature that this adds to the guts game is that if the kitty has the best hand at the table, everybody who went in loses and matches the pot. Now, the guts game ends when only one person goes in and beats the kitty. The kitty does not get a draw but it is not rare to see the kitty beat everybody at the table. The main advantage of the kitty is to eliminate the dealer advantage. If everybody before the dealer calls out, that dealer would normally win the game by default, calling in and having no other hands to beat. Now, that dealer would have to beat the kitty's hand in order to collect the pot. Otherwise, the pot is claimed by nobody and that dealer matches the pot. In Guts games that involve a draw, always include a kitty.

The Coin Declare

One way of calling in or out is by simply going in sequence after the dealer, starting with the player to the dealer's left and ending with the dealer. The disadvantage to this is that a player's decision is based on who called in or out previously, as opposed to all players declaring in or out at the same time. The coin declare is a method whereby all players declare at the same time. All players hide both hands and a chip (or coin) under the table, bringing up one closed hand over the table. If the player wants to go in, then he or she has placed the chip in this hand to be dropped on the table. If the player wants to go out, the chip remains in the hand that is not raised over the table. At the count of three, all players open their hands over the table. Those who drop the chip have declared themselves in, the rest are out.

PREPARING

BASICS

DRAW

STUD

GUTS

COMMUNITY

HOLD'EM

CASINO

NON-POKER

GLOSSARY

It's All Guts

A Guts theme can be added to just about any Poker game, especially Draw games. The dealer simply states that the game (Snowmen and Hockey Sticks, for example) requires before the draw that each player declare in or out. Those that are out are out of the game until it is re-dealt. Those that are in are allowed a draw (the betting round is optional) and of them, the one with the best hand collects the pot, while the rest match it. When a Guts game involves a draw, the dealer must determine, when players match the pot, if the players match the amount that it is there after betting occurred, or the amount that was in the pot at the time that player declared in. For example, the pot of a Draw Guts game started at five dollars but was increased by a dollar of betting among those players who declared in. The dealer must state whether the players that remained in must match the initial five dollar pot or the increased six dollar pot. This decision should be made before the hand is dealt.

Everybody Ante

This variation, which can be added to any Guts game, holds that with each new round of the game, every player re-antes into the pot. Under normal rules, the pot only increases in size when at least three players go in. The first collects the pot, the second matches the pot, and the third doubles the size of the pot. In Everybody Ante however, the pot increases at least by the size of every players' ante with each round. This variation is used primarily in Guts games that tend to end quickly, and require being spiced up. In addition, the dealer may also determine that the winner of the last round is not required to re-ante, but all other players must.

Best Hand Pays

This variation, which can be added to any Guts game, holds that if no player enters the pot, then all players must show their hands to the rest of the table. The player who has the best hand must ante for everyone before the game is re-dealt, which doubles the size of the pot. The variation is meant to punish the player who had the best hand at the table and didn't enter the pot with it.

Basic Guts

The dealer deals two cards to each player. If both cards in the player's hand match, then that player has a Pair. Otherwise, the hand is called simply by the high card between the two. For example, a King and an Eight would be a King-high. Beginning to the left of the dealer, each player decides whether or not they will go in or out. Those players who are out have no further stakes in the game unless it is re-dealt. Of those players who are in, the one with the best hand collects the pot while the others who called in throw into the pot the amount of money that the winner has collected. If the pot was worth 50 cents, then the winner collects that 50 cents while the other players, who called in but lost, put 50 cents into the new pot. If three players go in, then one player collects and two players match the pot, which would now be one dollar.

The game is then re-dealt by the player to the dealer's left and the same format continues. This game ends when one player goes in. That player collects the pot and the game is over.

This is the basic version of Guts Poker, from which all guts games stem. A few of the variations that follow can also be added to any Guts game. In this way, just about any Draw Poker game can be turned into a Guts game, simply by adding the stipulation that players must call in or out before the draw and betting round. Those players calling in are allowed a draw but risk matching the pot.

PREPARING

BASICS

DRAW

STUD

GUTS

COMMUNITY

HOLD'EM

CASINO

NON-POKER

GLOSSARY

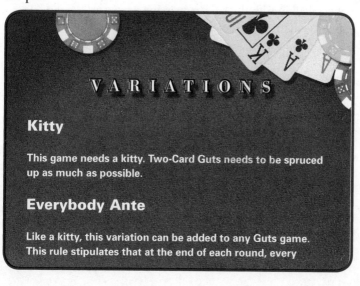

VARIATIONS

Kitty

This game needs a kitty. Two-Card Guts needs to be spruced up as much as possible.

Everybody Ante

Like a kitty, this variation can be added to any Guts game. This rule stipulates that at the end of each round, every player except the player who won the last round must re-ante into the pot on top of those players who had to match the pot from the round before. If ante is a nickel and there are six players, then the five players who did not win the previous round (whether or not they called in) raise the amount in the pot by a quarter each round. This is especially useful in basic Two-Card Guts.

Monte Carlo

Three cards are dealt to each player. Going in sequence around the table, starting with the player to the dealer's left, players call in or out. Those players that call in, without any kind of draw or betting round, throw down their three-card hands. The player who called in with the best hand at the table wins the pot, the others who called in match the pot. The game is re-dealt and ends when only one player calls in on a hand.

Monte Carlo is the fancy name for Three-Card Guts. Unlike Two-Card Guts, there are more possible hands than a High card or Pair, but unlike poker games that feature more cards, there are not as many possible hands. Being limited to three cards means no Two Pairs, Full Houses, or a Four-of-a-Kinds. A player can, however, put together the obvious High Card and Pair, as well as a Straight, a Flush, a Straight Flush, or a Three-of-a-Kind. A Straight in Monte Carlo is three cards in sequence; for example, a Nine-Ten-Jack. A Flush is three cards of the same suit; for example, a player who is dealt three Diamond-suited cards. A Straight Flush is three cards in sequence that are of the same suit. Monte Carlo follows its own ranking of hands that works as follows:

1) High Card
Nothing matches up or amounts to anything in the player's hand. The highest card in the player's hand is the High card. For example, if the highest card is a King, the player has King-high.

2) Pair
The player has two cards that match. For example, a pair of Queens.

3) Straight
Three cards in sequence, regardless of suit.

4) Flush
Three cards of the same suit, regardless of sequence.

5) Three-of-a-Kind
The player has three cards that match. For example, three Sevens.

6) Straight Flush
Three cards that are in sequence and that are all of the same suit. For example, a Four-Five-Six, all in Spades.

PREPARING

BASICS

DRAW

STUD

GUTS

COMMUNITY

HOLD'EM

CASINO

NON-POKER

GLOSSARY

Some tables take different opinions on what beats what between a Three-of-a-Kind and a Straight Flush, some tables favoring a Three-of-a-Kind as the best possible Monte Carlo hand. The dealer or house rules must determine which is better of the two.

Poker hand ranks are based on the probability of a certain hand being made. The hands that are statistically harder to achieve should be the better hand. Based on this logic, not only should the Straight Flush beat the Three-of-a-Kind, but a regular Straight should beat a Flush. In this case, the sequence would be:

• High Card
• Pair
• Flush
• Straight
• Three-of-a-kind
• Straight Flush

It is of utmost importance that the dealer clarifies this order before it is dealt.

VARIATIONS

Two and One

This one is an expensive game where players, for the most part, do not know what they are betting on. Two and One is the same as Monte Carlo, except players are dealt only two cards. To get a third card, a player must call in. Those players who call out do not get the third card dealt to them as they are out of the game. Those players who called in flip over their two card hands. The dealer then flips a card from the deck face-up to each two-card hand that called in, making a three card hand that follows the Monte Carlo what-beats-what table. When this game is dealt with a kitty, the kitty is always dealt its third card.

Kryptonite
courtesy nickiii@concentric.net

This is played as Monte Carlo with a kitty. One card in the kitty is turned face-up for the table to see. That card is wild in all hands, including in the kitty, giving it an automatic pair. Players must beat the kitty as well as each other. If nobody goes in, everybody must re-ante and the same kitty remains in the center of the table with the same wild card. Except that an additional kitty is dealt entirely face-down. Players must now beat both kitties. Everytime all players go out, an additional kitty is dealt.

3*5*7

This is a longer Guts game to play. To win the pot, a player must win the game five times (or five legs), although you may wish to reduce this number.

Everybody antes, and an ante a little larger than normal is called for. All players are dealt three cards. Threes are wild. Starting to the left of the dealer, players declare in or out. The twist in this game works as follows: if you declare out, but the player immediately after you declares in, then you are given the chance to change your mind. However, a player that declares in must stay in.

The players who called in exchange and look at each other's hands; the players who are out do not see anybody's hand. The player with the losing hand pays the player with the winning hand an amount equal to what is in the pot. This money does not go into the pot. It is paid directly from the loser to the winner.

Everybody is dealt two more cards. Threes are no longer wild, but Fives are now wild. There is another declare round, with the players who are in looking at each others' hands, and the loser paying the winner.

Everybody is dealt two more cards. Fives are no longer wild, but Sevens are now wild. Another declare round follows, and this time, players who are in can expose their cards to the table since everybody is about to be dealt new cards. The loser pays the winner.

The cards are collected and the game is re-dealt, starting back at three cards. Players re-ante the same amount as before.

PREPARING

BASICS

DRAW

STUD

GUTS

COMMUNITY

HOLD'EM

CASINO

NON-POKER

GLOSSARY

Without betting rounds, you can see now why the ante has to be a little larger.

As noted, a player must win five legs to collect the pot. The only way to win a leg is to be the only player who declares in on a declare round. That player does not win any money at that time since there is no losing player, but wins one leg. The first player to five legs wins the pot.

Jacks and Piss

Four cards dealt, plus a fifth community card in everyone's hand. This is Guts Poker with a draw. Jacks are always wild, plus the card turned up after the deal.

The dealer deals four cards to every player at the table, after which the top card on the deck is flipped over. That card, the "piss card" is not only wild, but it is also the fifth card in everyone's hand. If a Three is flipped, then it is wild in everyone's hand as well as all other Threes. Jacks are always wild. If a Jack is flipped up, then only Jacks are wild and hands will not be as good. In the following hand for example:

PISS CARD

The Ten of Hearts was flipped over as the piss card. One hand holds the Ten of Diamonds and the Jack of Spades. With a Ten as the Piss Card, the Ten in the hand is wild, as well as the Jack, which is always wild. Considering that the Piss Card is to be considered the fifth card in the hand, the hand consists of three wild cards. Put them together with the Ace of Clubs to make

Four-of-a-Kind with Aces. If this seems like a high hand, the amount of wild cards in this game, not to mention that the piss card guarantees you have a wild card in your hand right away guarantees high hands at the table most of the time.

After the deal, players decide if they want to stay in the game and risk matching the pot. Players declare in or out starting at the left of the dealer and going in clockwise order with the dealer calling last. Those players that call out are out until the next round of cards are dealt.

Those players that stay in are allowed a draw of as many cards as they want. After the draw, there is a betting round with all players who remained in the game. After the betting round, the player with the best hand collects the pot. All other players who stayed in throw into the new pot however much money was in the pot when they declared in.

If there is any money in the pot (in other words, if at least two people went in on the previous round) then the player to the left of the dealer deals the next hand and the same sequence continues. The game is dealt round after round until only one player goes in. That player collects the pot and the game is over.

PREPARING

BASICS

DRAW

STUD

GUTS

COMMUNITY

HOLD'EM

CASINO

NON-POKER

GLOSSARY

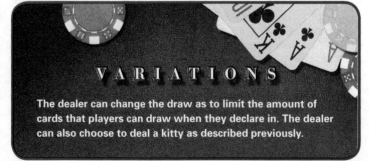

V A R I A T I O N S

The dealer can change the draw as to limit the amount of cards that players can draw when they declare in. The dealer can also choose to deal a kitty as described previously.

Indian Poker

This is not a game for everybody due to its simplicity and lack of any relation to actual poker. This politically-incorrectly named game involves each player putting a card on their forehead.

The dealer deals a single card to each player. At the same time, players raise the card to their forehead, but not so they can see it. The card is placed face-out on their forehead so that each player can see everybody else's card but their own. There is a declare round, where each player calls in or out on the strength of every-body else's cards. Everybody who calls in throws down their card. Whoever has the highest card collects the pot. Everybody else who called in matches the pot and the game continues.

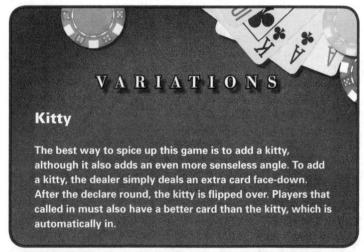

VARIATIONS

Kitty

The best way to spice up this game is to add a kitty, although it also adds an even more senseless angle. To add a kitty, the dealer simply deals an extra card face-down. After the declare round, the kitty is flipped over. Players that called in must also have a better card than the kitty, which is automatically in.

Three to Five

This is five-card Guts with only three cards initially dealt to each player. Players receive their fourth and fifth cards only if they call in.

The dealer deals three cards to each player. Either by clockwise declare or chip declare, players decide if they are in or out of the game. Those players that remain in the game are each dealt two extra cards to make their five card poker hand.

A round of betting is opened by the player to the dealer's left for all players who are in. After the betting round is the showdown. The best five card hand wins the pot, all other players that went in match the pot.

PREPARING

BASICS

DRAW

STUD

GUTS

COMMUNITY

HOLD'EM

CASINO

NON-POKER

GLOSSARY

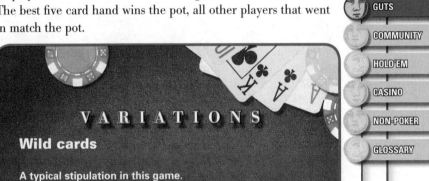

VARIATIONS

Wild cards

A typical stipulation in this game.

Kitty

If a kitty is dealt, it is always dealt its fourth and fifth cards after the declare round.

Thirty Eight

This is played the same as Three to Five, except for two variations.

1) Threes and Eights are wild.

2) Instead of betting, the player to the left of the dealer is the first to decide if he or she will call single, double, or triple. Single the pot is already what players must pay if they do

103

not win the hand. Next, in clockwise order, as in a betting round, players can decide to stay in the game, which now means risking double or triple what is in the pot. Once double or triple is called, subsequent players decide if they will remain in the game with that potential loss, or fold and simply pay single.

Example hand

On a $1 pot, players 1, 2, 5, and 6 go in. After the fourth and fifth cards are dealt to each player, Player 1 calls single, Player 2 calls double (now, the potential loss is $2), Player 5 folds and gets $1 ready, while Player 6 accepts the double. Player 1 calls triple (now, the potential loss is $3), Player 2 accepts the triple, and Player 6 folds and gets $2 ready. With each player having either seen or folded, Players 1 and 2 proceed to showdown.

Consecutive Guts

Five cards are dealt to each player. Players declare in or out. Those players that declared in compare hands. The best hand collects the pot, with the other players that went in matching the pot.

At the game's end, each player makes the best three-card hand of the five cards. However, players are able to use two cards in their hand as a single wild card if those two cards are consecutive. For example, if a player has Five-Jack-Four-Jack-Two, the Four and Five are consecutive and therefore act as a single wild card. Combined with the Jacks, this makes a hand of three Jacks.

Unlike Monte Carlo, there are no Straights or Flushes, leaving only High Card, Pair, or Three-of-a-Kind as possible hands. The game ends when one player goes in.

PREPARING

BASICS

DRAW

STUD

GUTS

COMMUNITY

HOLD'EM

CASINO

NON-POKER

GLOSSARY

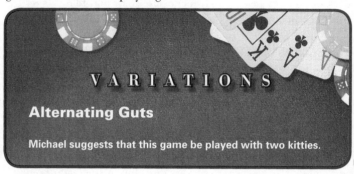

VARIATIONS

Alternating Guts

Michael suggests that this game be played with two kitties.

Four-Three

Everybody antes. Four cards are dealt to each player. After a declare round, those players that are in are dealt three additional cards.

Another declare round follows for players that are in, indicating if they are going High, Low, or both. Players use their best five card poker hand of the seven cards. Players calling both may use different combinations of five cards for High and Low. The winning High hand takes half the pot. The winning Low hand takes the other half. Those that are in but don't win either must match the pot.

VARIATIONS

Feel free to insert a betting round after the additional three cards are dealt and before the second declare round.

105

Wolfie's Lou

Five cards are dealt to each player. There is a free draw from the deck of up to two cards. Players declare in or out. Elan suggests the coin-declare.

Those players who are in play a version of Liar's Poker (without the lying) with an open round of asking who can beat given hands. For example, "Who can beat a pair?" "Who can beat a straight?". Players who can't meet the requirement are out of the running, but don't worry, they're not out of the hand yet. The player who ends up declaring having the best poker hand gets to call trump. For players not familiar with trump, it is a designated suit called in games where players must follow the lead (the first card played in a hand). When a player has none of the suit that has been led, he or she is free to play a card from the trump suit which automatically takes the trick. The only thing that beats a trump is a higher trump.

That player can call a suit as trump, no-trump, or can determine reverse no-trump, which isn't a suit but rather means that Twos are high, followed by Threes, etc. The lead is to the left of the dealer. Players must follow suit if they can. High card or high trump takes the trick.

A player must take three tricks to take the pot. Players that take only one or two tricks must match the pot. As a variation, players that take no tricks must double the pot.

Lying during the Liar's Poker round is cheating. The player who declares the best hand is kept honest to that hand. It should be considered cheating, but you may prefer something a little more flavorful, like tripling the pot.

PREPARING

BASICS

DRAW

STUD

GUTS

COMMUNITY

HOLD'EM

CASINO

NON-POKER

GLOSSARY

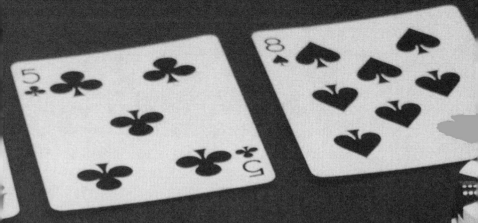

COMMUNITY POKER

Community games involve a certain number of cards dealt face-down to each player, as well as a certain number of cards laid out in the center of the table. These cards are flipped over as the game progresses, with betting rounds between the flipping of cards. Players put together their best five card hand by combining some or all of the cards dealt to them with some of the community cards that have been dealt in the center of the table. The purpose of these community cards is that they are shared amongst the players. Two players, for example, may make use of the same community cards in order to complete their hands. The one big difference between one Community game and the next is the format in which community cards are laid out on the table. The more common Community games involve the community cards being laid out in a line, a cross, or a circle, although the variations are endless. As cards are flipped over either one at a time or several at a time, it is normally at the dealer's discretion which cards get flipped, as he or she is the one doing the flipping. It has been said that the only thing that distinguishes one Community game from the next is the geometric shape in which the cards are laid. For this reason, stipulations are usually needed to spice up a Community game.

The Line

This format of community cards is more common in the Hold 'Em **games**, played by big-shot casino and big money tournament goers. It simply involves a line of cards flipped either one at a time or a few at a time and used in conjunction with the cards dealt to a player to make the best five card hand.

Another common line game is Cinncinati, which involves no more than 3 cards dealt to each player and a line of 4 cards in the center of the table, flipped one at a time. Players use these seven cards to make their best five card hand.

The Cross

This format of community cards involves rows of cards that intersect at some point, the most popular being Iron Cross. This typically involves a card that acts as the cross-point between rows of cards, this card being part of each row. There is normally a stipulation regarding that one card. It can be wild. In other instances, the player who is dealt the highest card of the same suit as the cross-point card wins half the pot. For example, if the cross-point card is the Two of Hearts, then the player who is dealt the highest Heart gets half the pot, the other half going to the player with the best hand at the table. For this reason, it is normally good form that the dealer flips that center card last. If it is wild or if the highest of its suit gets half the pot, the game is far more exciting when it is the last card flipped.

The Circle

This format is not as common. It involves a loop of cards, flipped over one at a time or several at a time by the dealer. The stipulation, as in Merry Go Round, is normally that cards in the loop used by players must be adjacent to each other. That is, if a player uses three cards from the circle of cards in conjunction with his hand, those three cards must be side-by-side on the circle.

Betting

The prominent feature of Community games are the rounds of betting that ensue the flipping of each card. At most small stakes tables, the general rule is that for every card flipped face-up

PREPARING

BASICS

DRAW

STUD

GUTS

COMMUNITY

HOLD'EM

CASINO

NON-POKER

GLOSSARY

by the dealer, there is a round of betting. One way that betting rounds can work is with the player to the left of the dealer, called the sucker, opening each of these betting rounds, as there are no cards showing as in Stud games. However, with games like H-Bomb that involve many betting rounds, another way is to have the opening of the betting round shift around the table in clockwise order for each card flipped. In other words, the first betting round is opened by the player to the dealer's left. The second betting round is opened by the player sitting 2 seats to the left of the dealer, and the third round by the player 3 seats to the left of the dealer, etc. The benefit of the latter method is that it does not put the pressure on one player to open each of several betting rounds.

High / Low
Many people enjoy adding this element to a Community game. As in Stud games, High/Low involves dividing the pot in two at the end of the game, half of it going to the player with the best hand, the other half going to the player with the worst hand. This feature keeps more players in the game longer.

Roll 'Em
The dealer may also decide to add more betting rounds to the game by requiring players to "roll" their cards in the hole. After all of the community cards have been flipped, and on the dealer's count of three, players flip over a face-down card of their choice. The best card showing opens a betting round, after which each player flips over a second card. The next betting round is opened by the best hand showing. This continues until each player only has one card remaining face-down. There's a final betting round, then the showdown.

THE GAMES

PREPARING

BASICS

DRAW

STUD

GUTS

COMMUNITY

HOLD'EM

CASINO

NON-POKER

GLOSSARY

Cincinnatti

One of the original Community Poker games, this is played with the dealer dealing five cards to each player. After this, the dealer lays out four or five (depending on how the dealer determines the game will be played) community cards in the center of the table. These cards are flipped one at a time, followed each time by a betting round. There is a final betting round after the last community card is flipped face-up, followed by the showdown. Players make the best five card hand out of the nine or ten cards.

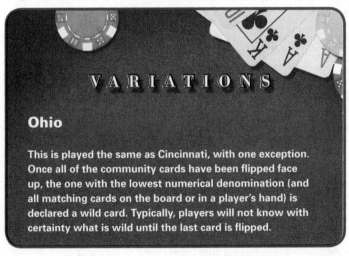

VARIATIONS

Ohio

This is played the same as Cincinnati, with one exception. Once all of the community cards have been flipped face up, the one with the lowest numerical denomination (and all matching cards on the board or in a player's hand) is declared a wild card. Typically, players will not know with certainty what is wild until the last card is flipped.

Tennessee

This is played the same as Cincinnati, but with fixed betting. The first betting round can only opened with a bet of one unit, that is one nickel at a nickel table or one quarter at a quarter table. The dealer determines the value of a single unit before the hand. A raise on the first betting round is limited to two units; no more, no less. An open on the second betting round can only consist of two units, and a raise, four units. A three unit open and six unit raise on the third, and a four unit open and eight unit raise on the fourth.

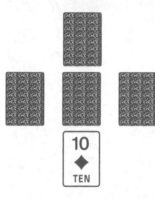

Iron Cross

Each player is dealt four cards. The dealer then lays five cards face-down on the table in two rows of three cards that cross each other at the center card of each row (see image). The dealer decides before the deal if that center card is wild. These cards are then flipped one at a time, followed by a betting round each time, making five betting rounds altogether. Once all five cards have been flipped (the center card is typically the last one flipped) and the fifth and final betting round is done, player decide which row of three cards are used to supplement the four cards in their hand. With these seven cards, the player makes the best five card hand.

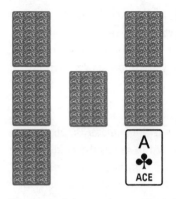

H-Bomb

All players are dealt four cards each. The dealer then lays seven cards face-down on the table in the shape of an H, that is two parallel rows of three cards, with a seventh card in the center connecting the two rows. A card on the H of the dealer's choice is flipped face-up right away, followed by a betting round.

The rest of the cards are flipped one a time, the card flipped at the dealer's discretion. After the flipping of each card, there is a round of betting, making seven rounds of betting altogether. Etiquette dictates saving the middle card for last, but the order in which cards are flipped is at the dealer's discretion.

Once all seven cards have been revealed, there is a final betting round. Each player matches the four cards in their hand with any of the five rows made up by the 'H', that is one of the two vertical rows, the horizontal row, and the two diagonal rows. Players then make the best five-card hand with these seven cards.

Pyramid

All players are dealt four cards each. The dealer then deals six cards face-down in the center of the table in the shape of a triangle. The peak of the triangle consists of one card, the next layer, of two cards, and the base, of three cards.

PREPARING

BASICS

DRAW

STUD

GUTS

COMMUNITY

HOLD'EM

CASINO

NON-POKER

GLOSSARY

Community cards are flipped one at a time. At showdown, players make their best five card hand with the four cards dealt to them, the peak card, one of the two middle layer cards, and one of the three base cards. In other words, players choose one card from each of the three rows to complement the four cards dealt to them.

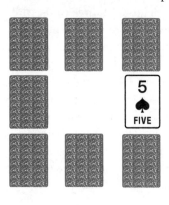

No Holds Barred

Just as the game of Baseball was created to satisfy the poker player who watches excessive baseball, No Holds Barred was apparently created to satisfy the poker player who is an avid viewer of professional wrestling. Four cards are dealt face-down to each player. Eight community cards are laid out in the center of the table in the shape of a square. These cards are flipped over one a time, followed by a betting round after each card flipped. Players use the four cards in their hand in conjunction with any three adjacent cards in the square, that is any three cards that are side-by-side, to make the best five card hand.

Some players play this game where the four cards on the corners of the square are wild. These cards, called "turnbuckle cards", are only wild when they are used in a player's hand. If a Ten is turned up on the top right corner, but a player chooses three cards that do not include that Ten, then that Ten is not wild in the player's hand. It stands to reason that hands will be high in this game, especially when players can choose a string of three cards that include two turnbuckle cards, hence two wild cards. As with most High/Low games, do not play this as High/Low if the turnbuckle cards are wild.

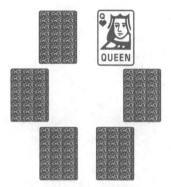

Merry Go Round

Four cards are dealt face-down to each player, followed by six community cards laid face-down in front of the dealer in the shape of a circle. The first of these community cards of the dealer's choice is flipped over, followed by a betting round opened by the player to the dealer's left. The second of these six community cards is flipped over, followed by another betting round. The dealer can determine that all betting rounds will be opened by the sucker (a term designating the player that must open every betting round in a game) to his or her left, or that the responsibility of opening each betting round circulates around the table every time a card is flipped.

The game is over when all six community cards have been flipped over, followed by a betting round after each one. Each player combines the four cards dealt to them with any three cards in the circle that are adjacent to each other. The three cards chosen by the player must be touching each other, that is they must be subsequent in the circle. Of these seven cards, players make their best five card hand.

Merry-Go-Round is a far more tame name for this game than its other name, Death Wheel. The game was probably given the latter name by its first player, as figuring out your hand at the end of the game can be a long, unpleasant process. Once all six cards are flipped, nobody ever knows what they have. Some people just see all bets and figure out what they have when it comes time to call.

PREPARING

BASICS

DRAW

STUD

GUTS

COMMUNITY

HOLD'EM

CASINO

NON-POKER

GLOSSARY

Rockleigh

Five cards are dealt face-down to each player, after which the dealer deals eight community cards face-down in the center of the table. These eight cards are dealt in two columns of four cards in each column, creating four sets of two cards.

The dealer chooses one pair of the four, and flips both cards face-up, followed by a betting round. The dealer then flips up a second pair, following by a betting round, followed by a third pair, betting round, fourth pair, final betting round.

Players make their hand with the five cards dealt to them and any one pair of community cards of the four set pairs. This is not to say any two of the community cards, but rather any set pair of community cards as the dealer has dealt four pairs.

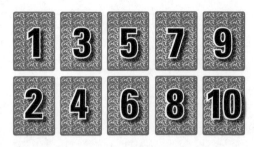

PREPARING

BASICS

DRAW

STUD

GUTS

COMMUNITY

HOLD'EM

CASINO

NON-POKER

GLOSSARY

Twin Beds

Four cards are dealt to each player, followed by ten community cards dealt face-down on the center of the table, as shown here. The dealer immediately flips over cards 1 and 2, which is followed by a betting round. Cards 3 and 4 are flipped over, followed by another betting round. Continue to flip over two cards and follow it with betting rounds until all cards are revealed.

Players make their best five card hand from the four cards dealt to them and additional cards from one row or the other. Players cannot use community cards from both rows.

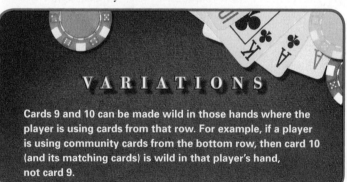

VARIATIONS

Cards 9 and 10 can be made wild in those hands where the player is using cards from that row. For example, if a player is using community cards from the bottom row, then card 10 (and its matching cards) is wild in that player's hand, not card 9.

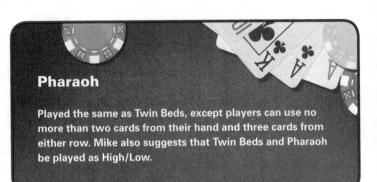

Pharaoh

Played the same as Twin Beds, except players can use no more than two cards from their hand and three cards from either row. Mike also suggests that Twin Beds and Pharaoh be played as High/Low.

The Spoiler

Five cards are dealt to each player, followed by five community cards dealt face-down on the center of the table in any layout. One community card is flipped, followed by a betting round. A second community card is flipped, followed by another betting round, then a third community card is flipped, followed by another betting round.

After the third betting round, players must discard three cards from their hand. The last two community cards are flipped one at a time, followed by a betting round. Players make their best five card hand using the five community cards and the two cards left in their hand.

The Good, The Bad, and The Ugly

Five cards are dealt to each player, followed by ten community cards face-down on the table in two rows. The dealer designates one row as the good row, and the other as the bad row.

The dealer flips up two adjacent cards, one from each row. Any player with a card matching the one that was flipped from the bad row must discard that card. A betting round follows. Two more cards are flipped, followed by another betting round, and players discarding their cards that match those turned up in the bad row.

If a card appears in both rows, then the bad row overrules the good row, and those cards are discarded.

After all of the cards have been flipped over, and there has been a final betting round, the dealer flips the top card on the deck. If its value is Two-Seven, then the lowest hand at the table wins the pot. If its value is Eight-Ace, then the highest hand wins the pot.

Bingo

Four cards are dealt to each player, followed by nine community cards face-down on the table in a 3 x 3 square. The dealer flips one card over at a time, followed by a betting round.

Players use their four hole cards in conjunction with any row of community cards, horizontally, vertically, or diagonally, to make their best five-card poker hand. Best hand wins.

PREPARING

BASICS

DRAW

STUD

GUTS

COMMUNITY

HOLD'EM

CASINO

NON-POKER

GLOSSARY

VARIATIONS

Scratch and Win

This is played the same as Bingo, except an additional row is dealt separate from the square of cards. This row is flipped all at once before showdown.

Hold 'Em Poker is basically Community Poker combined with the use of blind bets in place of antes. The main Hold 'Em game from which all others branch is Texas Hold 'Em.

In addition to designations of minimum bet and maximum bet, in Hold 'Em Poker (with the exception of Home Hold 'Em) another designation is made for the "small blind" and the "big blind" bets. Instead of starting off the pot with antes, Hold 'Em games start with two blind bets (bets made by players before they even see their cards). The small blind should be slightly less than or equal to the minimum bet. The big blind should be twice as much as the small blind.

Before looking at his or her cards, the player to the left of the dealer places the small blind bet into the pot and the player to the left of the small blind does the same with the big blind bet. The player to the left of the big blind is the first player who can actually look at his or her hand before deciding whether or not to call the blinds, see the blinds and raise, or fold. The rest of the betting round proceeds as a regular poker betting round, bearing in mind that the two blinds have already invested money into this betting round and only need to see the bumps that were made after them.

This applies only to the first betting round. All other betting rounds proceed as per regular poker betting rounds, following the flipping of the community cards. The standard number of community cards in a Hold 'Em game is five. Three cards are flipped after the first betting round ("The Flop"), a fourth after the second betting round ("The Turn") and a fifth after the third betting round ("The River").

Winning Percentages Of Starting Hold 'Em Hands

These rankings are the result of computer simulations involving no betting, raising, or folding. They are the pure result of starting hands held through a round to a showdown. While fairly accurate in a no fold 'em hold 'em (low-limit) scenario, these numbers can't be used with complete accuracy in a live game situation as the winning percentages could definitely change through betting patterns and split pots.

PREPARING

BASICS

DRAW

STUD

GUTS

COMMUNITY

HOLD'EM

CASINO

NON-POKER

GLOSSARY

RANK	HAND	OCCURRENCE	WINS
1	AA	0.45%	31.00%
2	KK	0.45%	26.02%
3	QQ	0.45%	22.03%
4	AKs	0.30%	20.19%
5	JJ	0.45%	19.09%
6	AQs	0.30%	18.66%
7	KQs	0.30%	18.08%
8	AJs	0.30%	17.47%
9	KJs	0.30%	17.05%
10	TT	0.45%	16.83%
11	AK	0.91%	16.67%
12	ATs	0.30%	16.63%
13	QJs	0.30%	16.58%
14	KTs	0.30%	16.14%
15	QTs	0.30%	15.84%
16	JTs	0.30%	15.78%
17	99	0.45%	15.29%
18	AQ	0.91%	14.87%
19	A9s	0.30%	14.60%
20	KQ	0.91%	14.43%
21	88	0.45%	14.16%
22	K9s	0.30%	14.15%
23	T9s	0.30%	14.07%
24	A8s	0.30%	13.89%
25	Q9s	0.30%	13.82%
26	J9s	0.30%	13.80%

RANK	HAND	OCCURRENCE	WINS
27	AJ	0.91%	13.45%
28	A5s	0.30%	13.43%
29	77	0.45%	13.36%
30	A7s	0.30%	13.35%
31	KJ	0.91%	13.18%
32	A4s	0.30%	13.17%
33	A3s	0.30%	13.07%
34	A6s	0.30%	12.97%
35	QJ	0.90%	12.89%
36	66	0.45%	12.77%
37	K8s	0.30%	12.77%
38	T8s	0.30%	12.73%
39	A2s	0.30%	12.69%
40	98s	0.30%	12.63%
41	J8s	0.30%	12.47%
42	AT	0.90%	12.43%
43	Q8s	0.30%	12.42%
44	K7s	0.30%	12.23%
45	KT	0.90%	12.23%
46	55	0.45%	12.15%
47	JT	0.91%	12.13%
48	87s	0.30%	12.02%
49	QT	0.91%	11.99%
50	44	0.45%	11.94%
51	22	0.45%	11.93%
52	33	0.45%	11.86%
53	K6s	0.30%	11.84%
54	97s	0.30%	11.74%
55	K5s	0.30%	11.57%
56	76s	0.30%	11.47%
57	T7s	0.30%	11.47%
58	K4s	0.30%	11.40%
59	K2s	0.30%	11.27%
60	K3s	0.30%	11.26%
61	Q7s	0.30%	11.20%
62	86s	0.30%	11.16%
63	65s	0.30%	11.13%

RANK	HAND	OCCURRENCE	WINS
64	J7s	0.30%	11.12%
65	54s	0.30%	10.90%
66	Q6s	0.30%	10.85%
67	75s	0.30%	10.69%
68	96s	0.30%	10.65%
69	Q5s	0.30%	10.55%
70	64s	0.30%	10.44%
71	Q4s	0.30%	10.43%
72	Q3s	0.30%	10.42%
73	T9	0.90%	10.38%
74	T6s	0.30%	10.31%
75	Q2s	0.30%	10.28%
76	A9	0.91%	10.20%
77	53s	0.30%	10.18%
78	85s	0.30%	10.12%
79	J6s	0.30%	10.10%
80	J9	0.90%	9.99%
81	K9	0.90%	9.93%
82	J5s	0.30%	9.86%
83	Q9	0.91%	9.81%
84	43s	0.30%	9.81%
85	74s	0.30%	9.74%
86	J4s	0.30%	9.73%
87	J3s	0.30%	9.57%
88	95s	0.30%	9.56%
89	J2s	0.30%	9.50%
90	63s	0.30%	9.49%
91	A8	0.91%	9.42%
92	52s	0.30%	9.25%
93	T5s	0.30%	9.23%
94	84s	0.30%	9.14%
95	T4s	0.30%	9.11%
96	T3s	0.30%	9.06%
97	42s	0.30%	9.02%
98	T2s	0.30%	8.97%
99	98	0.91%	8.97%
100	T8	0.90%	8.93%

PREPARING

BASICS

DRAW

STUD

GUTS

COMMUNITY

HOLD'EM

CASINO

NON-POKER

GLOSSARY

RANK	HAND	OCCURRENCE	WINS
101	A5	0.91%	8.92%
102	A7	0.90%	8.83%
103	73s	0.30%	8.75%
104	A4	0.90%	8.72%
105	32s	0.30%	8.70%
106	94s	0.30%	8.70%
107	93s	0.30%	8.53%
108	J8	0.91%	8.50%
109	A3	0.91%	8.50%
110	62s	0.30%	8.48%
111	92s	0.30%	8.46%
112	K8	0.90%	8.45%
113	A6	0.90%	8.39%
114	87	0.91%	8.36%
115	Q8	0.90%	8.28%
116	83s	0.30%	8.23%
117	A2	0.90%	8.18%
118	82s	0.30%	8.11%
119	97	0.90%	7.96%
120	72s	0.30%	7.91%
121	76	0.90%	7.88%
122	K7	0.90%	7.86%
123	65	0.91%	7.57%
124	T7	0.91%	7.53%
125	K6	0.91%	7.46%
126	86	0.91%	7.40%
127	54	0.90%	7.36%
128	K5	0.91%	7.13%
129	J7	0.91%	7.10%
130	75	0.90%	7.01%
131	Q7	0.90%	6.97%
132	K4	0.91%	6.95%
133	K3	0.90%	6.87%
134	96	0.91%	6.77%
135	K2	0.91%	6.76%
136	64	0.90%	6.75%
137	Q6	0.91%	6.58%

RANK	HAND	OCCURRENCE	WINS
138	53	0.90%	6.57%
139	85	0.91%	6.30%
140	T6	0.90%	6.28%
141	Q5	0.91%	6.26%
142	43	0.91%	6.17%
143	Q4	0.91%	6.13%
144	Q3	0.91%	6.05%
145	74	0.90%	5.96%
146	Q2	0.91%	5.95%
147	J6	0.91%	5.94%
148	63	0.91%	5.73%
149	J5	0.91%	5.63%
150	95	0.91%	5.60%

HAND	OCCURRENCE	WINS
HIGH CARD	17.41%	0.01%
ONE PAIR	43.83%	1.67%
TWO PAIRS	23.50%	8.92%
THREE-OF-A-KIND	4.83%	33.56%
STRAIGHT	4.62%	33.36%
FLUSH	3.03%	46.88%
FULL HOUSE	2.60%	52.74%
FOUR-OF-A-KIND	0.17%	86.27%
STRAIGHT FLUSH	0.03%	91.73%

PREPARING

BASICS

DRAW

STUD

GUTS

COMMUNITY

HOLD'EM

CASINO

NON-POKER

GLOSSARY

Texas Hold 'Em

The Pre-Flop

Two cards are dealt face down to each player. Before (or while) they are being dealt, the player to the dealer's left makes the pre-determined "small blind" bet. This is immediately followed by the player to the left of the small blind making the "big blind" bet.

The player to the left of the big blind is the first player permitted to look at his or her hand before making a betting decision. That player can call the big blind, see the big blind and raise, or fold. The rest of the betting round conducts itself as a regular poker betting round, with the opening bet to call, raise, or fold.

When the betting round reaches the small blind, it must be noted that that player has already invested a sum of money into this betting round. Technically, it was the small blind that opened this betting round by making the initial bet. Whatever the amount of the betting round when it reaches the small blind, the amount of the small blind bet is what that player has already invested into this betting round.

The same goes for the big blind. If nobody bumps the bet after the big blind, then the big blind owes nothing as this was the player that made the last bet. It must be noted, however, that contrary to regular poker betting, if nobody bumps the bet after the big blind, the big blind owes nothing, but is still allowed the option to bump the betting round when it reaches him or her. If the big blind declines from bumping, then the betting round is over.

The Flop
Burn the top card of the deck (put it with mucked cards). The next three cards from the deck are flipped face up in the center of the table. The small blind opens a second betting round, which proceeds as a regular poker betting round.

The Turn
Burn another card, then the next card from the deck is flipped face up in the center of the table as the fourth community card. The small blind opens a third betting round, which proceeds as a regular betting round.

The River
Burn one last card, then the next top card from the deck is flipped face up in the center of the table as the fifth and final community card. The small blind opens a fourth and final betting round, which proceeds as a regular betting round. After this betting round, players make their best five card hands using the two cards in their hand and the five community cards in the center of the table.

PREPARING

BASICS

DRAW

STUD

GUTS

COMMUNITY

HOLD'EM

CASINO

NON-POKER

GLOSSARY

Hold 'Em Strategy
Position
One of the keys to sound Hold 'Em play is understanding the value of a player's position in relation to the dealer. Players who are closer to the right side button have a distinct advantage over players who are to the dealer's left. In Hold 'Em, the betting begins at the small blind, the first position to the left of the dealer. These players are under the gun, and must be the first to act. Any action they make gives their opponents an opportunity to make a judgment about their hand before they must respond. For this reason, the dealer position is extremely desirable as you can get a read of the entire table before you must act. A shrewd player can often steal pots with a late position raise, or get off easy when the action gets too hot to handle. When you find yourself towards the button, or on it, you can afford to take chances you wouldn't normally take if you were forced to bet first.

Flop vs. Turn

After the flop, bets in Hold 'Em increase substantially. In a $3/$6 game, the bets before and at the flop are $3, but at the turn and river cards, it's $6. If you're holding an average hand, stick around to see a flop when no raise is present, if it improves, consider playing on the turn. If you don't get hit by the flop, it's best to fold.

Slowplaying

No matter how bad your hole cards, there's always the chance that you could flop a monster. When you find that you've miraculously flopped a full house, straight or flush, it may be best to slowplay a good hand and make a strong bet at the turn. Let the flop action go by with a check or call, then make it expensive for other players to stick around on theTurn. When you've flopped a very strong hand, a good slowplay can prove profitable, whereas a bet on a weak flop can scare away the other players. Suffice to say, the Turn and River bets count, if you're drawing dead, get out after the flop.

Starting Hands

One of the fundamental concepts of Hold 'Em is that you usually have the option to fold your hand before you've paid a cent. There are some hands that are hopeless, and Hold 'Em usually gives you the opportunity to throw them away for free. While it's tempting to stay in on some low cards, you must consider how many possibilities the board can make for your hole cards. If you're playing Jack Six, remember that when the board shows up Queen Jack Five, you have only the second best possible hand despite your pair of Jacks. Any player holding a Queen has you beat. Be aware of the impact of the board on your hand and the potential of better hands to be out there. You're safe to see a flop with any high card with a good kicker, (Ace-Nine, King-Ten, Queen-Eight), a high pocket pair (Eights or better), good suited cards (King-Five, or any suited Ace), connecting cards (Six-Seven, Nine-Ten) or any obvious monster (Ace-King, King-Queen, King-King, Ace-Ace). When you find yourself holding a big hand in the hole (pocket Aces, Kings, Queens, Jacks, Ace-King, suited Ace, high suited connecting cards) make a raise pre-flop. This allows you to get the pot big early while you still have an advantage. Once the flop hits, hands can change dramatically, when you have a hand that is strong, you generally want to play it strong.

PREPARING

BASICS

DRAW

STUD

GUTS

COMMUNITY

HOLD'EM

CASINO

NON-POKER

GLOSSARY

Playing the Nuts

On the Turn and River, if you know you have the best possible hand on the board, you want to play aggressively. Make sure that a player that is drawing to beat you on the Turn or River is forced to pay for the opportunity to beat your hand. Giving them free cards with a check, or making it cheap for them to see more cards will not help hold up your hand. When you have the nuts at the Turn or River, bet and raise the nuts! If someone is betting back into you, even better, don't back down, mentally confirm that you've got the best hand, and raise them back.

Playing the Blinds

While the blind bets are at a disadvantage by virtue of their position, they do have some advantage in that they have some disguise as to the strength of their hand. These two forced bets, when no raise is present, are made at least in part regardless of the strength of the player's hole cards. So, when the action goes around the table, the blinds are the last to act pre-flop giving them the best opportunity to get in the last word. After the flop comes, the blinds are under the gun. So pre-flop, a blind raise can often steal a pot when the table checks around.

VARIATIONS

Home Hold 'Em

One variation is played the same as Texas Hold 'Em, with the one exception that there are no blind bets. Each player antes into the pot as per regular poker. There is no small blind or big blind, all betting rounds are started by the player to the left of the dealer and as per regular poker betting rounds.

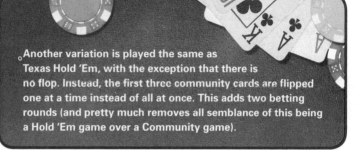

Another variation is played the same as Texas Hold 'Em, with the exception that there is no flop. Instead, the first three community cards are flipped one at a time instead of all at once. This adds two betting rounds (and pretty much removes all semblance of this being a Hold 'Em game over a Community game).

Omaha Hold 'Em

This is played the same as Texas Hold 'Em, with two exceptions. One, each player is dealt four cards at the beginning of the game instead of two.

Two, when making the best five card hand, players must use exactly three of the five community cards and two of their four hole cards. The game can be played with Texas Hold 'Em rules (with blinds) or with Home Hold 'Em rules (with antes).

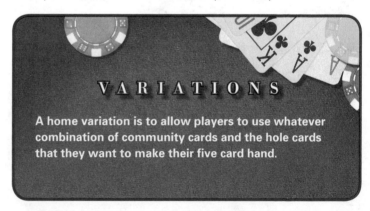

VARIATIONS

A home variation is to allow players to use whatever combination of community cards and the hole cards that they want to make their five card hand.

PREPARING

BASICS

DRAW

STUD

GUTS

COMMUNITY

HOLD'EM

CASINO

NON-POKER

GLOSSARY

Omaha Hi-Lo Split

This is played the same as Omaha Hold 'Em, with two exceptions.

One, the game is played as High/Low. After the betting round following the River, the pot is split between the player with the highest hand at the table, and the player with the lowest hand at the table. The dealer or House needs to determine if High and Low needs to be declared in clockwise order before showdown (or if "cards speak"), and if a player is permitted to call "Both" using different five-card combinations of his or her nine cards.

Two, that in order to win Low, a player must have no higher than an Eight down. If no player has an Eight or less down, then the game is played as All-High.

Irish Hold 'Em

This is played the same as Omaha Hold 'Em, with one exception.

After seeing the first three community cards on the flop, each player must discard two of their four cards. The rest of the game is played with players using the five community cards and the two cards left in their hand.

Super Eight

This is played the same as Texas Hold 'Em, with the one exception that each player is dealt three cards at the beginning of the game instead of two.

Tahoe

This is played the same as Super Eight, with the one exception that each player can only use two of their three hole cards in their final hand.

Pineapple

This is played the same as Super Eight, with the one exception that players must immediately discard one of their three hole cards between the first betting round and the flop.

Crazy Pineapple

This is played the same as Pineapple, with the one exception that players discard one of their hole cards after the flop and before the second betting round.

PREPARING

BASICS

DRAW

STUD

GUTS

COMMUNITY

HOLD'EM

CASINO

NON-POKER

GLOSSARY

Progressive Hold 'Em

This is played the same as Texas Hold 'Em, with two exceptions.

There are no blinds. It is optional that each player ante before any cards are dealt.

Players set up four stacks of chips in front of them. The size of the stacks is determined by the dealer before the game is dealt. The recommendation is stacks of $0.50, $1, $1.50, and $2. After the first two cards are dealt, each player can either fold or push their first stack into the pot. After the flop is turned up, each player can either fold or push in their second stack. After the turn is flipped up, each player can fold or push in their third stack. After the river is flipped up, each player can fold or push in their fourth stack. Finally, there's the showdown and the best hand wins.

There is an obvious positional advantage to this game as there is no betting or raising, but rather a "Let It Ride" type of decision to fold or stay in for the price. There are two options to overcome this advantage for the dealer:

1) The first action to stay in or fold rotates so that it isn't always the player to the dealer's left, or

2) The coin declare.

CASINO POKER

THE THEME

Without question, many home poker players frequent casinos. For the most part, it ends up being that once-a-month experience where somebody is willing to put up quite a bit more at a casino on a wider variety of games than one would at the home poker table. Every now and then, such a home poker player may call a casino-played game, adapting it to the home poker table.

Calling a "casino game" at the home poker table poses only one problem, but one that is assumed by the dealer who calls the game. That dealer, most of the time, must play as the House, meaning players are no longer playing against each other, but rather as individuals playing against the dealer. The dealer plays against each player and at the end of the hand, either paying each player's bet or collecting that player's bet.

Take the classic Blackjack, for example. The dealer who calls Blackjack deals everyone a hand, including one for the House. The dealer plays that hand against each individual player's hand. Players are no longer bluffing in the hopes of being that single player who collects the pot, but are up against the House. There isn't even the camaraderie of teaming together against the dealer. Instead, players are concerned with nothing more than the hand dealt to them and the one dealt to the dealer.

There are no standard variations or features with casino games, each one is unique and played differently. The beauty of converting it from a casino-business game to a home poker game is that the dealer specifies what the rules are and how it differs from the game played in the casino. The dealer may choose to play the game exactly as it is played in the casino, or with so many variations, that it truly resembles a home poker game. The sad part, and what is considered blasphemy by some, is that many of these are not even poker games. Some of them, like Blackjack, do not even play with a poker theme.

PREPARING

BASICS

DRAW

STUD

GUTS

COMMUNITY

HOLD'EM

CASINO

NON-POKER

GLOSSARY

Let It Ride

The game begins with each player placing three equal antes. This ante is determined by the dealer and agreed upon by the players. Three cards are dealt face down to each player and two community cards are placed face down in front of the dealer.

At this time, each player, in clockwise order, determines if they will remove one of their three antes from the table based on the cards they have received. Only one of the three antes may be removed, or players "let it ride," meaning that ante remains on the table. A removed ante goes back in the player's stack, which is a safe move. However, in the case of a winning hand at the end of the game, it's money for which the player is not paid. Players who choose to let it ride cannot remove that ante later in the game.

The dealer flips one of the two community cards, and players have the option to remove the second of their three antes from play. Again, players who choose to let it ride cannot remove that ante later in the game. There is no opportunity to remove the third ante.

The dealer then flips the second community card, and the game is over. Each player's hand is made up of their three cards in conjunction with the two community cards to make their five card hand. Any player whose hand consists of a pair of nines or worse loses the antes left on the table. Any player whose hand consists of a pair of tens or better will get paid on each of the antes that they have left on the table, based on the following pay-out table:

ROYAL FLUSH	1,000 to 1
STRAIGHT FLUSH	200 to 1
FOUR OF A KIND	50 to 1
FULL HOUSE	11 to 1
FLUSH	8 to 1
STRAIGHT	5 to 1
THREE OF A KIND	3 to 1
TWO PAIR	2 to 1
PAIR OF TENS OR BETTER	1 to 1

What is interesting is that players are paid on each of the antes that they have left on the table. If a player has one ante of fifty cents on the table and gets a pair of Jacks, that player is paid fifty cents by the dealer. However, player with the same hand and two antes on the table gets one dollar from the dealer.

Strategy

Pull back those bets where you can't win as soon as possible, but leave your options open when you can draw to a big payout. When your 3 cards don't reveal a high Pair, Flush or Straight draw, pull back those bets! If you have a hand with some possibility, let the first bet ride, and pull back a bet if you don't get hit by the card the dealer flips. Remember that only Tens or better pay on Pairs, so low cards only pay with trips.

PREPARING

BASICS

DRAW

STUD

GUTS

COMMUNITY

HOLD'EM

CASINO

NON-POKER

GLOSSARY

Pai Gow Poker

Pai Gow Poker is a game adapted from an old Chinese dominoes game. In other words, if you ask twenty people how to play Pai Gow Poker at the home poker table, you won't get the same answer twice. What follows are different ways that Pai Gow can be played at a home game.

The dealer must first designate the stakes. On each play, the dealer either pays a player for his hand, collects from the player, or there is a push. At a nickle or quarter table, the stakes usually involve bets of up to $2. There are no betting rounds so the amount bet is the only amount of money that a player stands to win or lose. However, the dealer must also bear in mind that every player may bet maximum and win. A dealer who calls a $2 maximum with 5 players stands to win or lose up to $10, while individual players stand to win or lose up to $2.

Seven cards are dealt to each player and the dealer. The players and the dealer make two hands out of these seven cards, one hand of five cards and one hand of two cards. The five card hand plays out as a regular poker hand. The two-card hand is played out as a Two-Card Guts hand, consisting of either a high card or a pair.

The only stipulation regarding the division of these seven cards is that the five card hand must be better than the two card hand. In other words, if the two card hand consists of a Pair, then the five card hand must consist of at least a Pair of the same value. For example, the hand cannot turn into a Pair of Aces in the two card hand and five mismatched cards in the five card hand.

Play begins with each player placing their two-card hands face-up. The dealer's two-card hand is exposed next. Every two-card hand beat by the dealer is turned face-down. Players next expose their five-card hand, followed by the dealer's five-card hand. Each player's five-card hand that does not beat the dealer's is flipped facedown.

For every player that has both of hands flipped face-up, the dealer pays even money to the bet that player made. For every player that has both hands flipped face-down, the dealer collects that player's bet. For every player that has one hand flipped up and one flipped down, it is a push. The player's bet is simply returned. In other words, beating the dealer on both hands collects; losing to the dealer on both hands pays; winning one and losing the other is a push.

VARIATIONS

PREPARING

BASICS

DRAW

STUD

GUTS

COMMUNITY

HOLD'EM

CASINO

NON-POKER

GLOSSARY

What is described previously is the closest to the Pai Gow that is played in casinos. However, it often makes for an unexciting home game. Players who are unsure of the game or their hands will make small bets and in the end, not win or lose a great deal. Check out Pai Gow in the Stud Poker section for versions more home-game-friendly, where players play each other instead of the House.

Use the same betting concept, except determining the win or loss comes down to the five card hand. Players make their bets after dividing their seven cards and exposing their two-card hands. The players whose two-cards hands are not as good as the dealer's are automatically out, their bets collected by the dealer. Those players remaining for the showdown of five card hands may add to their bets if they wish. Next, all players and the dealer expose their five-card hands. Those players with better hands than the dealer are paid even money, including the amount that they bumped up their bet. The dealer collects the bets from the rest of the players.

Red Dog

Red Dog is how In-Between is played in the casinos. The dealer plays as the House, but is not dealt cards. Each player places a bet and is dealt two cards face-up. Starting with the player to the left of the dealer, each decides whether or not to add money to their original bet based on the first two cards. An extra wager can be added to the original bet up to the total of the original bet.

For example, an original bet of fifty cents can have up to fifty cents added to it.

Following this decision, if the player's two cards match, then the dealer deals the player a third card. If that third card is also a match, the player is paid eleven times his or her bet. If that third card does not match, then it is a push. If the player's two cards are consecutive, then it is an automatic push. If the player's two cards neither match nor are consecutive, the dealer announces "the spread" before the player adds anything to the original bet. The spread represents the amount of numbers that fall between the player's two cards. For example, if the player's two cards are a Five and a Nine, then it is a three-card spread, as only Six, Seven, and Eight fall between those two cards.

Players then choose how much they wish to add to their original bet. The player is then dealt a third card. If the player's third card falls between the first two cards, he is paid by the dealer based on the following pay-off table:

1-CARD SPREAD	pays 5:1
2-CARD SPREAD	pays 4:1
3-CARD SPREAD	pays 3:1
ALL OTHER SPREADS	pays even money, 1:1

If the player's third card matches either of the first two or does not fall in between the first two numerically, that player's bet is collected by the dealer.

In the game of In-Between, players whose third card matches either one of their first cards has "hit the post" and must pay double their bet. No such rule exists in Red Dog. A player whose third card matches either of the first two cards simply loses the amount bet.

Caribbean Stud Poker

Before any cards are dealt, each player places a bet in front of them. This can range from the table's minimum bet to its maximum bet. However, based on the rules of the game, the dealer may decide to alter the stakes somewhat. Five cards are dealt to each player and the dealer. However, one of the cards dealt into the dealer's hand must be face-up (hence, Caribbean Stud), whereas all other cards are dealt face-down.

Players then determine if they will stay in the game or not, somewhat Guts-style. This happens, starting to the left of the dealer and moving in sequence around the table. Players indicate that they will stay in the game by adding an equal sum of money to their original bet. If their original bet was for 50 cents, then to stay in the game, they must add an additional 50 cents to that original bet. Those that call out are out of the game, and their original bets collected by the dealer, acting as the House.

Once players have determined whether they are in or out, the remaining four cards in the dealer's hand are flipped. If the dealer's hand is not at least as good as an Ace-King, that is, if the dealer's hand does not consist of at least a pair, then all remaining bets at the table are paid even money and the hand is over. If the dealer's hand is at least as good as an Ace-King, that is, consisting of a pair of Twos or higher, then the dealer's hand is compared against each player's hand at the table. If the dealer's hand beats a player's hand, then the dealer collects that player's bet, both the original bet and the double-up bet. If the dealer's hand loses to a

PREPARING

BASICS

DRAW

STUD

GUTS

COMMUNITY

HOLD'EM

CASINO

NON-POKER

GLOSSARY

player's hand, then the dealer pays even money to that player's bet. Additionally, players may be awarded an extra sum of money by the House based on their hand.

1 PAIR EVEN MONEY	the player is paid the same amount that was bet
2 PAIRS 2 TO 1	paid double what was bet
3 OF A KIND 3 TO 1	paid triple what was bet
STRAIGHT 4 TO 1	paid quadruple what was bet
FLUSH 5 TO 1	paid five times what was bet
FULL HOUSE 7 TO 1	paid seven times what was bet
4 OF A KIND 20 TO 1	paid twenty times what was bet
STRAIGHT FLUSH 50 TO 1	paid fifty times what was bet
ROYAL FLUSH 100 TO 1	paid one hundred times what was bet

VARIATIONS

The Stakes

Like any other casino game, this one comes down to stakes. The dealer determines these stakes, bearing in mind how much he or she stands to lose. If the stakes are not high enough, the game will probably not go over well. If the stakes are too high, the dealer's wallet may be in danger.

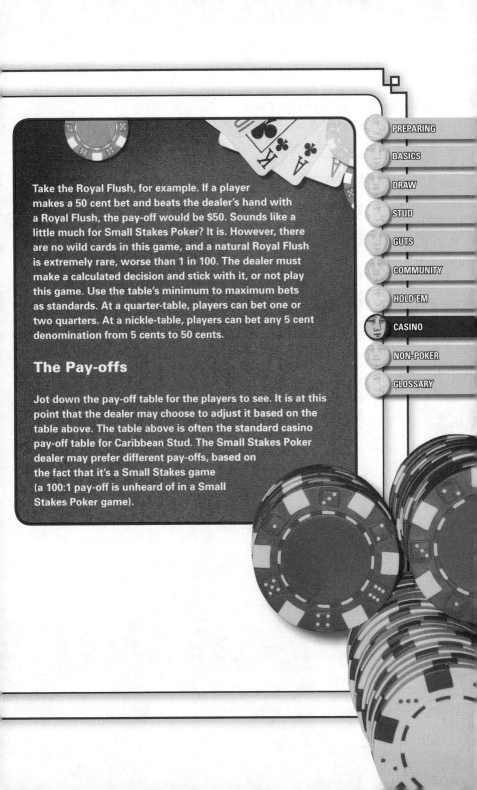

PREPARING

BASICS

DRAW

STUD

GUTS

COMMUNITY

HOLD'EM

CASINO

NON-POKER

GLOSSARY

Take the Royal Flush, for example. If a player makes a 50 cent bet and beats the dealer's hand with a Royal Flush, the pay-off would be $50. Sounds like a little much for Small Stakes Poker? It is. However, there are no wild cards in this game, and a natural Royal Flush is extremely rare, worse than 1 in 100. The dealer must make a calculated decision and stick with it, or not play this game. Use the table's minimum to maximum bets as standards. At a quarter-table, players can bet one or two quarters. At a nickle-table, players can bet any 5 cent denomination from 5 cents to 50 cents.

The Pay-offs

Jot down the pay-off table for the players to see. It is at this point that the dealer may choose to adjust it based on the table above. The table above is often the standard casino pay-off table for Caribbean Stud. The Small Stakes Poker dealer may prefer different pay-offs, based on the fact that it's a Small Stakes game (a 100:1 pay-off is unheard of in a Small Stakes Poker game).

NON-POKER GAMES

THE THEME

Oddly enough at the Home Poker table, games get called that have nothing to do with poker. These non-poker games are played because they involve a deck of cards and a sum of money on the line. While this meets the requirements for most home gamblers, not every table allows them as some are more ridiculous than others. There are of course, plenty of non-poker games worth playing when your game gets stale.

THE GAMES

7/27

This is a numbers game. The value of cards in this game are face value except for Aces, which the player can choose to make One or Eleven, and face cards, which are worth a half a point. When the game ends, the pot is split between the player whose hand is closest to a number value of Seven and the player whose hand is closest to a number value of Twenty-Seven.

Each player is dealt one card face-down and one card face-up, followed by a betting round. In clockwise order beginning to the dealer's left, the dealer asks players if they would like to receive another card. When the dealer has made a complete round of the table, if at least one player chose to take an extra card, there is another betting round. Following the betting round, the dealer again asks players if they will take an additional card. If at least one player takes one, then this is followed by another betting round.

A player is allowed to decline from taking an additional card on one turn, then accept an additional card on a subsequent turn. However, once a player declines on taking an additional card three times, that player's hand is frozen, and no longer permitted to take additional cards.

Once the dealer makes the round of the table and no player chooses to take an additional card, there is a final betting round. What follows is a declare round, with players declaring whether they are going for the best Seven Hand or the best Twenty-Seven Hand. Of those declaring "Seven," the player whose hand's number value is closest to seven receives half the pot. Of those declaring "Twenty-Seven," the hand closest to twenty-seven receives the other half the pot.

Before the game starts, the dealer must announce how to break tied hands. An example tie hand would be if two players declare "Seven," one with a hand worth six, the other with a hand worth eight. The dealer may announce that "the low tie hand wins." In this example, the hand worth six wins, or "the high tie hand wins." In this example, the hand worth eight wins. The last alternative is "tie hands split their half of the pot."

A hand consisting of two Aces and a Five is the perfect hand, and one that automatically wins both halves of the pot. A player may call "Pig," declaring both the best "Seven hand" and the best "Twenty-Seven hand," but it would not be too wise unless that player had the two Aces and Five.

PREPARING

BASICS

DRAW

STUD

GUTS

COMMUNITY

HOLD'EM

CASINO

NON-POKER

GLOSSARY

Bing Bang Bong

Each player positions three antes in front of him or herself and is dealt seven cards. The player to the dealer's left leads a card. The following player reveals one of his or her cards, and this continues with each player revealing single cards in clockwise direction.

If the card revealed by a player matches the card played by the previous player, then the previous player owes one of his or her antes into the pot. For example, if Player A plays a Six, Player B plays an Eight, then Player C plays another Eight, then Player B owes an ante into the pot (Bing). Furthermore, if Player D were to play another Eight, then Player C owes two antes into the pot (Bing Bang). Furthermore, if Player E plays the fourth Eight, then Player D owes all three antes into pot (Bing Bang Bong). Annoying players even say the "Bing", "Bing Bang", and "Bing Bang Bong" as it happens throughout gameplay.

Players continue revealing single cards from their hands, throwing in an ante when the following player plays a matching card. When a player has run out of his or her three antes, that player is out of the game. What this means is that a Bing Bang Bong automatically removes a player from gameplay.

When all players have run out of cards, the deck is re-shuffled, either by the initial dealer or a following player, and seven cards are again dealt to each player still in the game. When a single player has an ante or more remaining, that player wins the whole pot.

Strategy

Count cards. Remember what you have seen so that you can play cards with more confidence that the following player does not have a matching card. If you are leading early and are holding a pair, play one of them. It is more likely that the following player does not have a matching card.

Lou (Bourre)

Three cards are dealt to each player. A trump card is flipped, and the game is played Guts style. Those players who go in get a draw of as many cards as they want. On the play, players must follow suit. Each trick is worth a third of the pot. Each player who goes in and does not get at least one trick must match the pot.

This game is difficult to classify because it is Guts style, it has a draw, but because there is trump and the goal is to collect tricks, it was classified under Non-Poker Games. The dealer must first decide on the ante, which must be at least 15 cents. The reason for this is because the pot must be divisible by 3, so a nickel-ante table would have a 15-cent ante for this game. The pot is divided into 3 equal piles. Three cards are dealt to each player and a trump card is flipped. The cards are going to be played by players throwing out one of their cards at a time in sequence, and always following suit if they can. For those unfamiliar with trump, it automatically takes the trick, unless a higher trump card is thrown on the same round. If Spades is trump, Hearts were led, and everybody has a Heart but you, you can throw down any Spade and it gets you the trick. If another player also did not have hearts, he or she could play a higher Spade to take the trick.

As it is Guts, players must call in or out. The best way to do this is with the chip declare, where players lower one chip or coin under the table with both hands, raising only one hand over the table. Players who choose to go in have the chip in their hand. Those who do not want to go in leave the chip in the hand that is not raised over the table. Once each player has one hand raised over the table, all players open that hand at the same time. Those that drop a chip are declaring in. These players are allowed a draw of as many cards as they want.

PREPARING

BASICS

DRAW

STUD

GUTS

COMMUNITY

HOLD'EM

CASINO

NON-POKER

GLOSSARY

Play ensues with the first player who called in to the left of the dealer leading. Each player in this game must follow suit, meaning playing a card of the same suit as the first played, if possible. Otherwise, they may throw down a trump card if they have one to try to take the trick. Once all players who went in have played their three cards, players take a third of the pot for each trick collected. Those players that went in and did not collect at least one trick of the three must match the pot. If two players went in and collected no tricks, then the pot doubles, but is still divided into three piles for the next round. The game ends when each player who went in collects at least one trick. Otherwise, somebody will be throwing money into the pot and the player to the left of the dealer re-deals the same game.

VARIATIONS

A different way to determine who leads, rather than it simply being the player who calls in to the left of the dealer, works in the following fashion. The number on the card that is flipped up is the number of spaces counted starting to the left of the dealer and counting only those players who went in. If a Four was turned up, then 4 spots are counted after the dealer among those players who went in to determine who leads.

Another variation has each trick not worth a third of the pot. Rather, those players that went "in" and only collected 1 trick match the pot, as well as those players who collected no tricks. The player who collects 2 or 3 tricks collects the entire pot.

Chase the Ace

One card is dealt to each player. Kings are high, Aces are low. After the deal, players decide whether they will keep their card or exchange with the person to their left. After this decision, the next player to the left has the same choice. When it comes to the dealer, the dealer can either keep the card dealt, or cut for a new one from the deck. The player with the lowest card at the table loses one of three turns.

First, the dealer determines how much money is at stake. Players have three equal piles of money in front of them, representing the three turns that they have in this game. At a low stakes table, it is typical that the three piles are three quarters or three piles of two quarters in each pile. The dealer must bear in mind that the winner of this long-winded game wins the total amount of money at the table, so it needs to be enough money that it is worth the time.

One card is dealt to each player. Aces are low, and Kings are high. The first player (Player #1) has the option to either keep the card dealt or exchange with the player to the left (Player #2). If Player #1 chooses to exchange, Player #2 has no choice but to exchange his or her card for Player #1's card. Player #2 now has the same choice, to either keep the card or exchange it with the player to the left. The game is called Chase the Ace because a player that is dealt an Ace will no doubt choose to exchange it, as will every player at the table who gets that Ace passed to them. Once the round of exchanging has reached the dealer, the dealer has nobody to exchange with. Therefore, the dealer can either keep the dealt card or cut for a new one from the remaining cards in the deck. After the dealer has made this choice, all players throw down their card. The player with the lowest card at the table

PREPARING

BASICS

DRAW

STUD

GUTS

COMMUNITY

HOLD'EM

CASINO

NON-POKER

GLOSSARY

throws the first pile of money into the center of the table as that player has lost the first round and now only has two rounds left. If two players have the same card and it is the lowest card at the table, then both players have lost the round and must put one of their piles into the pot.

The player to the left of the dealer deals the next round in the same fashion. When a player loses all three piles of money, he or she is out of the game and the other players continue. The game ends when there is only one player remaining, and that player collects the money that has accumulated in the center of the table. It is not that bad of a game, so long as it is only played once in the course of a night.

VARIATIONS

Grace or Welfare Round

Most tables play that each player has not 3 rounds but 4 rounds. When a player has lost all 3 piles, he or she is still in for one more chance, known as the Grace Round. A player on a Grace Round who loses another round is then out of the game.

King Stops Play

Another popular stipulation is that any player holding a King can throw it down face-up at any point in the round. This automatically stops the round and players are stuck with the card that they are holding when the King is thrown down.

This can be done to stop a particular
player from exchanging their card for another,
or to stop the dealer from cutting from the deck. The King
thrown down brings a complete stop to the round.

The Stayner Rule

This one stipulates that if it should happen that two players
remain and both of them on their Grace Round, if at the end
of their round, they are holding the same card, two jacks for
example, then the game is reset and replayed with every player
back in the game with three piles of money in front of them. The
money that had accumulated in the pot remains there and the
winner now wins twice as much as a normal game

Dealer Double Burn

If the dealer cuts from the deck and the cut results in the dealer
receiving the same card (for example, if a four is traded in and
the cut results another four) and if that card is the lowest at the
table, the dealer pays not once but twice.

In-Between (Acey Deucey)

Two cards are dealt face-up to each player. In order, each player
bets from nothing to however much is in the pot whether or not the
third card dealt face-up will fall numerically between the first two.
If the player wins the bet, that player collects the bet amount out of
the pot. If the player loses the bet, that player adds the bet amount
into the pot.

PREPARING

BASICS

DRAW

STUD

GUTS

COMMUNITY

HOLD'EM

CASINO

NON-POKER

GLOSSARY

The player does not need to bet. If a bet is made, that bet will be from the table's minimum denomination bet to the entire amount in the pot. After the bet is made, the dealer throws face-up the next card off the top of the deck. If, for example, the player is dealt a Two and a Ten, and the next card off the top of the deck is an Eight, that player collects the bet amount from the pot. If, for example, the next card is a Jack, that player pays the bet amount into the pot. Once the player has either declined betting, won, or lost, the dealer then deals a second card to the second player to the left and the same options apply. This sequence continues around the table, including the dealer who has the same options.

If the third card dealt to a player is the same as one of the first two (for example, the player has a Two and a Ten, and the next card is another Ten) then that player has not only lost the bet, but has hit the post. This player must pay double the bet amount into the pot. If, for example, the player bets everything that is in the pot and hits the post, that player must pay into the pot double the amount that is already in there, thus tripling the size of the pot.

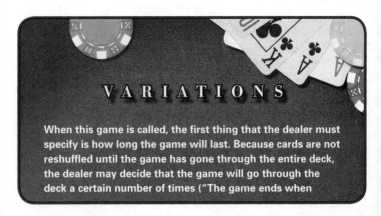

VARIATIONS

When this game is called, the first thing that the dealer must specify is how long the game will last. Because cards are not reshuffled until the game has gone through the entire deck, the dealer may decide that the game will go through the deck a certain number of times ("The game ends when

PREPARING

BASICS

DRAW

STUD

GUTS

COMMUNITY

HOLD'EM

CASINO

NON-POKER

GLOSSARY

we've gone through the deck three times."
for example). The dealer may decide that the game ends
when a player bets the pot and wins, thus emptying the pot.
The best formula is often a combination of both principles. A
good way to start is to specify that the game will go through
the deck at least twice, after which the game continues
until the pot has been cleared out. In this way, if the pot is
emptied before the game has finished going through the
deck, then every player, including the winner, simply re-antes
and the game continues. Another way to prolong the length
of the game is to call that players can only bet a maximum of
half-pot until the game has gone through the full deck once.

Ante

This all depends on the table and what everybody is willing
to put up to start. The bottom line is that the ante in In-
Between should be significantly higher than the normal
game ante. A good formula is to say that
the ante for In-Between is three times the usual
ante. If you are playing at a nickel-ante table, then ante for
In-Between would be 15 cents. If regular ante is a quarter,
then ante for In-Between would be 75 cents. Bear in mind
that if the dealer decides everybody must re-ante if the pot is
emptied before the game is finished, that this same amount
must be re-anteed by each player.

Indian Poker

Each player gets one card that the players place on their foreheads to see everybody's card but their own. Betting rounds
ensue and the highest card wins the pot.

159

See Indian Poker in the Guts section. This time-filler is usually called by the dealer who can think of nothing else. Players are reminded that they are not to look at their card, only lift it up, face-out and place it on their forehead. Done on the count of three, players can now see everybody's card but their own.

The dealer must determine how many betting rounds there will be. Since it's non-poker, the dealer may even determine that there is a draw of one card, separating two entire betting rounds. Whatever tactless ways in which the dealer spices up this one, the player who stays in the game and ends up having the highest single card at the table wins the pot.

It's a simple game, and makes for a funny scene when somebody who has never played it walks into the room and sees a table full of players holding cards on their foreheads. Check for reflective surfaces before calling this game.

Gin Poker

Players are dealt five cards and draw single blind cards from the deck in clockwise order until one player believes he or she has the best poker hand at the table and knocks.

Players ante once, as there will be no betting rounds. The ante is typically a larger sum of money for this reason. Five cards are dealt face-down to each player. The remainder of the deck is placed in the center of the table. The dealer flips the top card from the deck face-up directly beside the deck. The player to the dealer's left has the option of picking up the face-up card or a blind card from the top of the deck. As players can never have more than five cards, that player must discard one of the six cards now in his or her hand. The player places this discard face-up where the initial face-up card is or was, as Gin Rummy is played.

The next player has the same option of a blind card from the deck or the top card on the discards next to the deck. This carries on around the table non-stop, with players discarding one card from their hand, so that each player only has five cards.

The goal is to put together the best possible five-card poker hand. When one player feels that his or her hand is the best poker hand at the table, that player knocks in place of drawing and discarding. Once a player knocks, each other player is allowed one more draw, after which all players expose their hands. The best poker hand wins the pot.

PREPARING

BASICS

DRAW

STUD

GUTS

COMMUNITY

HOLD'EM

CASINO

NON-POKER

GLOSSARY

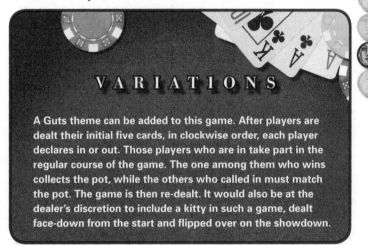

VARIATIONS

A Guts theme can be added to this game. After players are dealt their initial five cards, in clockwise order, each player declares in or out. Those players who are in take part in the regular course of the game. The one among them who wins collects the pot, while the others who called in must match the pot. The game is then re-dealt. It would also be at the dealer's discretion to include a kitty in such a game, dealt face-down from the start and flipped over on the showdown.

Curacao (Dutch) Stud
The dealer deals one card face up to each player at the table. If any two players have cards that match, all cards are collected and placed at the bottom of the deck. The dealer then deals another card face up to each player at the table, and continues to do so until each player has a different card face up.

The dealer then proceeds to deal one card at a time face up in the center of the table. If a card dealt face up in the center of the table matches any player's card, that player grabs it from the center of the table, adding it to his or her card. That player then opens a betting round.

The dealer continues to deal single cards face up in the center of the table. The player with that card takes it from the center of the table, and opens a betting round. The first player with Four-of-a-Kind wins half of the pot, and the game continues. The second player with Four-of-a-Kind wins the other half of the pot.

Put and Take

Players play against the dealer. For the Put Round, each player is dealt five cards face up, after which the dealer deals himself or herself one card face up. Any player with a card in their hand that matches the dealer's card antes once into the pot, equal to the table's ante/minimum bet amount. The dealer then deals himself or herself a second card. Any player with a matching card antes twice into the pot. Any player with a card matching the dealer's third card antes four times into the pot. Matching the dealer's fourth card results in eight times the ante into the pot. Matching the dealer's fifth and final card antes sixteen times into the pot.

The dealer then collects his or her five cards, placing them at the bottom of the deck.

For the Take Round, the dealer deals himself or herself one card. Any player with a matching card in their hand takes one ante from the pot. The dealer deals a second card. Any player with a matching card takes two antes from the pot. Any player with a card matching the dealer's third card takes four antes out of the pot. Any player with a card matching the dealer's fourth card takes eight antes out of the pot. Any player with a card matching the dealer's fifth and final card takes sixteen antes out of the pot.

When the Take Round has been completed, any money remaining in the pot is claimed by the dealer. However, if the pot is emptied before the end of the game, the dealer must pay the takes out of his or her own money.

Bingo
Everybody antes. Three cards are dealt face down to each player, as well as five cards dealt face down in the center of the table.

The dealer flips the first of the five cards in the center. Any player who has a card in his or her hand that matches the one that was flipped up must discard that card from his or her hand. Players do not receive a new card to replace the one that was discarded, and are now short at least one card. If a player has two cards that match the one that was turned up, both of those cards are discarded.

This is followed by a betting round opened by the player to the left of the dealer. After this betting round, a second of the five cards is flipped over, and again, any player holding a matching card must discard it. Each of the five cards are flipped over in this manner, each time followed by a betting round. After the fifth and final card is flipped, there is a final betting round.

The pot is splits between the player who has the highest numerical value of cards in his or her hand and the player who has the lowest numerical value of cards. To determine numerical value, each card counts as its face value, with Aces worth one or fifteen (player's choice), Jacks worth eleven, Queens worth twelve, and Kings worth thirteen.

PREPARING

BASICS

DRAW

STUD

GUTS

COMMUNITY

HOLD'EM

CASINO

NON-POKER

GLOSSARY

By either clockwise declare or chip declare, each player decides if they wish to go High, Low, or Both. Players can use one hand to go for Both by using an Ace differently in both hands. A player who was forced to discard his or her entire hand throughout gameplay automatically wins the Low half of the pot. Of those players that go High, the one with the highest numerical value wins half of the pot. Of those going Low, the one with the lowest numerical value, the other half of the pot.

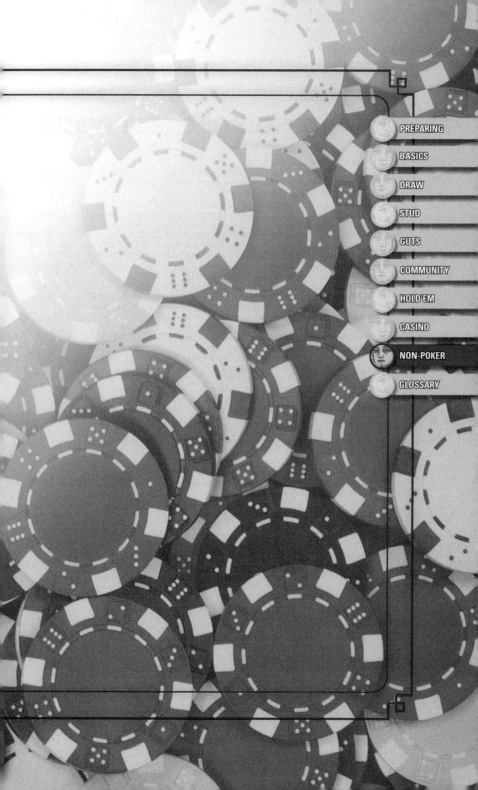

PREPARING

BASICS

DRAW

STUD

GUTS

COMMUNITY

HOLD'EM

CASINO

NON-POKER

GLOSSARY

GLOSSARY OF POKER TERMS

A

Ace: The highest-ranking card.

Ace High: A five-card hand containing an Ace but no pair. Beats a King, loses to a pair.

Aces Up: A hand with two pair, where one pair is aces, is said to be Aces Up

Acey Deucey: (a) Any game where Aces and Twos are wild.

(b) when a player's two cards or two cards showing are an Ace and a Two

Action: When it is a player's turn to make a decision, it is said to be that player's action; a hand with lots of betting is said to have good action.

Advertising: A strategy used to purposely give other players a false impression of how you play. It is typically performed early in the game and at an inexpensive opportunity. As a false sense of one's style is developed, this is exploited later at an opportunity when there is significant money to be won.

Aggressive: A style of play characterized by much betting and raising, making it expensive for other players to stay in the pot. See also Passive, Loose, and Tight.

Ahead: The amount of profit that has been made in a session. For example, "I'm ahead ten dollars."

All-in: When a player bets all of the money that he or she has on the table. Typically used in no-limit poker, where the only limit on a player's bet is the amount that he or she has on the table.

Ante: The amount of money that each player must throw into the pot before the game is dealt. It is the initial interest that each player has in the game before it is even begun, and is usually the same amount as the minimum bet at the table.

Ante Up: A dealer request for antes to be paid.

Anything Opens: In Draw, a game where there is no qualifier required to open the first betting round.

Art Gallery: A five-card poker card made up entirely of face cards.

B

Back to Back: Two paired hole cards, i.e. "Back to back Jacks."

Back Into, To: To end up with a hand other than the one originally anticipated. i.e. chasing a flush and backing into a straight flush.

Bad Beat: (a) A story told involving a poker hand gone awry; a story of bad luck or with an unfortunate ending.

(b) To suffer a large loss when playing a strong hand.

Bankroll: A players available funds are said to be his bankroll.

Behind: A player who has lost money is said to be playing behind.

Belly Hit: To complete an inside straight.

Bet: (a) To place a sum of money into the pot, either to open, to see and call, or to see and raise.

(b) the amount of money thrown into the pot.

Bet Into: To bet before a stronger hand, or a player who placed a strong bet on the prior round.

Bicycle Wheel: A straight made up of an Ace, Two, Three, Four, and Five. Otherwise called a Low Straight, the lowest possible Straight. Considered by some people to be the best hand in Lowball.

Big Blind: In Hold 'Em, this is the largest compulsory ante that is paid by the player two seats to the left of the dealer.

Blackleg: A nineteenth century term for a card player of ill repute.

Black Mariah: (a) A term used in the Seven-Card Stud game High Chicago where a player has the best hand at the table and the highest Spade face-down.

(b) a Seven-Card Stud game in its own right where the hand that wins the pot must be both the best hand and have the highest Spade face-down.

Blind: (a) In Hold 'Em, the pot is started with blind bets instead of antes. One or two players to the left of the dealer are required to make forced bets before even seeing their hands. As the deal rotates around the table, so too does the burden of having to make the forced blind bet.

(b) to check or bet before receiving or examining hole cards.

Blow Back: To lose back most or all of one's profits.

Blue: The color of poker chip most often used to represent the highest denomination of money. It's the source of the term "blue chip stock."

Bluff: The act of betting higher than one should with a particular hand, so players think you are holding a better hand than it is. A tactic used in the hopes that players with better hands will fold from the pot.

Board: These are the community cards in Hold 'Em and Community poker games. In Stud games, these are the cards dealt face-up in each player's hand.

Boat: A Full House.

Bobtail: An outside-straight.

Boss: The strongest hand at a betting round.

Brick: (a) In Stud poker, a card dealt face-up to a player that does nothing to help that player's hand.

(b) In Community poker, a community card that is flipped up that does nothing to help a player's hand.

Broadway: A Straight made up of a Ten, Jack, Queen, King, and Ace. Otherwise called a High Straight, the highest possible straight.

Buck: The term used to describe the dealer button which indicates which player represents the dealer in casino play; this player should receive the last card. It's the source of the phrase "The Buck stops here." See Button.

Bug: A Joker included in the game that can only be used as an Ace, or to complete a Straight or a Flush.

Bullet(s): An Ace or pair of Aces.

Bump: To raise.

Buried: A card that a player needs to complete a hand that does not end up being dealt from the deck is said to have been buried.

Burn: (a) Losing a round in a game based on rounds, ex. Chase the Ace; a double burn is when two players lose a round.

(b) the act of placing the top card aside face-down and out of play, an anti-cheat mechanism used in *Hold 'Em.*

Bust: A hand which has failed to improve.

Bust a Player: To eliminate a player from a tournament by taking all of his or her chips.

Busted: A player who is out of chips is busted.

Busted Flush/Straight: A flush or straight of only four cards.

Button: A plastic disc used in casinos where there is a house dealer to designate the player who would have otherwise been dealing if the deal were rotating. The player dealing the hand is said to be on the button.

Buy-In: The amount of money required to sit down at the table for a specific game.

By Me: An expression used to indicate that a player checks or folds.

C

Cage: A casino area, almost always behind bars where a player exchanges chips for cash.

Call: The act of seeing a bet and not raising it any further. Some home games require that the first player to call is the first player to show his or her hand at Showdown.

Calling Station: A player who always calls, and therefore cannot be bluffed.

Cap: (a) A limit placed on a Guts poker game to control how much money can be lost at one time; i.e. a five-dollar cap means that no player can win or lose more than five dollars at any given time.

(b) a limit placed on the number of raises that can be made in a betting round; i.e. many casinos employ a three-raise rule before the cap is reached.

Cards Speak: A house rule determining that players do not need to call their own hands. If a player miscalls a hand, the house corrects that player. The opposite of Players Speak.

Case Card: The last card of a denomination or suit, where the rest have been seen.

Cash In: To leave a game and change one's chips for cash with the dealer.

Cash Out: To leave a game and change one's chips for cash at the cage.

Catch: To have the card a player wanted to pull appear at a draw.

PREPARING

BASICS

DRAW

STUD

GUTS

COMMUNITY

HOLD'EM

CASINO

NON-POKER

GLOSSARY

Chase: When a player remains in the pot because his or her hand has the potential to improve to a better hand, that player is said to be chasing the better hand.

Check: (a) When the betting round has not yet been opened, a player who opts not to bet is said to check. The difference between this and a call is that in the latter instance, the betting round has been opened.

(b) A term for a chip.

Check-Raising: A player who checks on a betting round, but raises when a bet is put to him or her in the same round. Also known as Sandbagging.

Chicago: A Stud split-pot game where the pot is split between the player with the best hand and the player with the highest face-down Spade; otherwise known as High Chicago. A variant that splits the pot between the best hand and the lowest face-down Spade is known as Low Chicago.

Chip: A plastic, wooden or clay disc used to represent money.

Chop-Chop: To split a pot in the event of a tied hand.

Cinch Hand: A hand which cannot be beaten. See Nuts.

Close to the Vest, Playing: (a) Playing cautiously.

(b) holding one's cards close enough to oneself so that players on either side cannot see them.

Closed Poker: Any poker, typically Draw poker, in which all cards are dealt face-down.

Coffeehouse, To: To make reference to one's hand out loud at the table, whether being honest or not. This activity is banned in some home games.

Coin Declare: A method of declaring in Guts poker, where all players raise a closed hand over the table and open their hands at the same time; players who drop a coin or chip are declaring in, those who drop nothing are declaring out.

Cold: A streak of bad cards or luck.

Cold Deck: A deck of cards which has been set in advance by a cheat.

Come: To play a poor hand on the hopes of improving it. Source of the term "playing on the come."

Community: Any game where a certain number of cards are revealed to all players in the center of the table and can be used in conjunction by each player with the personal cards that were dealt to each player.

Community Cards: Those cards in a Community poker that are positioned in the middle of the table and are shared by all players.

Connectors: Cards of consecutive numeric value which may make a straight.

Court Card: Any face card: a Jack, Queen, or King.

Cowboy: A King.

Cut: To divide the deck into two piles and reverse their order after the shuffle, but before the deal.

D

Dead Card: A card which is no longer playable within the rules of a game.

Dead Hand: A hand which is no longer playable.

Dead Man's Hand: A hand consisting of both black Eights and both black Aces. The hand held by Wild Bill Hickok when he was shot in 1876.

Deadwood: The collection of cards near the center of the table, consisting of discards and folded hands.

Dealer-advantage: A factor in any game where there is an obvious advantage to the dealer somewhere in the rules and stipulations. For example, a Guts game without a Kitty allows the dealer the last declare. If all other players have declared out, the dealer automatically wins by declaring in.

Dealer's Choice: A house rule determining that the deal of cards is to move in clockwise order around the table from hand to hand, with the particular game played determined by that game's dealer. The dealer has full authority to call any game, and each player has full authority to agree to play the game or not.

Deceptive Play: Not to be confused with cheating; when a player bets in a way that does not correspond accurately to his hand. This takes the form of Bluffing, in that the hand is not as good as the bet indicates, or Slowplaying, in that the hand is better than the bet indicates.

Deck: A pack of fifty-two playing cards.

Declaration: The act announcing whether a player is attempting to win the high, low or both ends of a pot.

Default: To win a pot by default is to win only because there are no other players left in the game. The player winning by default is not obliged to show his or her hand, as nobody paid to keep that player honest.

Deuce: A Two.

Discard: The act of exchanging cards from one's hand for new cards from the deck.

Dog: The underdog, or player less likely to win a particular hand.

Door Card: The first card dealt to each player face-up in Stud poker, otherwise called Second Street in Five-Card Stud, and Third Street in Seven-Card Stud.

Down and Dirty: The last card made available to each player. In Hold 'Em, it is the fifth community card. In Stud, it is the seventh card dealt face-down to each player.

Down Cards: Hole cards, or any other face down cards.

Draw: (a) Any game where players have the opportunity to exchange a designated number of their cards for new cards from the deck.

(b) in games where there are more cards to come (Stud, Hold 'Em, Community), a hand with potential to improve to a better hand is said to be on a draw.

Drawing Dead: Drawing cards to a hand that cannot possibly win the pot, regardless of what cards are received on the draw.

Draw Out: To win a hand on the last card after playing an inferior hand.

Drop: To fold a hand.

F

Face Card: A King, Queen or Jack. See Court Card.

Family Pot: A pot in which all, or at least most, players have stayed in until the Showdown.

Fifth Street: In Hold 'Em, the fifth community card dealt. See River.

Fill: To receive the card needed to complete a hand.

Fish: A habitual loser. Also known as a Jobber, Chump, Monkey or Mark.

Five-of-a-Kind: Five cards of the same denomination; only possible in wild-card games.

Floorman: A card room employee supervising a group of tables.

Flop, The: The first three community cards dealt in Hold 'Em.

Fold: The act of withdrawing from a game due to a bet that is higher than the player cares to match in order to stay in the game. Also known as to Drop.

Fourflush: A hand that is four cards to a flush. Typically, these hands do not have any true value as a poker hand.

Fourth Street: In Hold 'Em, the fourth community card dealt. See Turn.

Flush: Five cards of the same suit. Beats a Straight, but loses to a Full House.

Free Ride: A betting round in which no player chose to bet, allowing everybody to remain in the game at no cost.

Freeze-Out: A term usually used to describe a tournament game where all players start with the same amount of chips and the winner is decided when one player holds all the chips.

Full House: A hand containing Three-of-a-Kind, and a Pair. Beats a Flush, loses to Four-of-a-Kind. In the case of two competing Full Houses, the higher Three-of-a-Kind wins.

G

G: One thousand dollars. Also known as a grand.

Go South With It: To pocket winnings in the middle of a playing session, with the intention of keeping it and not gambling it.

Guts: Any game that opens with players declaring whether or not they are in or out of the game. Of those players who declare in, the one with the best hand collects the pot, the others match the pot and the game is re-dealt. This type of game normally only ends when only one player declares in.

Gutshot: A term used to describe the card needed to fill an inside Straight.

H

Hand: (a) The collection of cards that a player is holding, making up a particular rank (e.g. Straight, Full House, etc.).

(b) a particular game or round of card-playing (ie. "That was a fun hand")

PREPARING

BASICS

DRAW

STUD

GUTS

COMMUNITY

HOLD'EM

CASINO

NON-POKER

GLOSSARY

Hard Rock: A particularly tight player.

Heads-up: When a game is reduced to two players, these players are said to be competing heads-up for the pot.

High/Low: (a) A stipulation added to any game, usually Stud games, where the pot is divided equally between the player with the best hand and the player with the worst hand

(b) a Seven-Card Stud game in its own right with no wild cards and with the pot split between best and worst hands.

High Roller: A player who gambles for large sums of money.

Hit: To receive a card one needs to improve a hand.

Hit and Run: A player who wins a large pot and quickly exits from the table and the poker-playing, as not to lose any of the money just won. Considered unethical.

Hold 'Em: A form of Community poker where some cards are dealt to each player and the rest are dealt in the middle of the table and shared by all players. There are five community cards with the first three flipped up together, followed by the fourth, followed by the fifth, with betting rounds in between. Texas Hold 'Em is the staple casino poker game, made popular as the featured game of the World Series of Poker.

Hole Cards: Cards dealt face-down in Stud or Hold 'Em games.

Honest, To Keep: To call another player's bets in case they are bluffing to ensure that they do not win the pot by default. Also called paying to see, in that if a player wins a pot by default, he or she is not obliged to show his or her hand because nobody paid to see it.

House, the: (a) The game's host. Also known as the Keeper.

(b) the place in which the game is being played.

House Rules: The written or assumed rules and regulations that govern the specific play of poker in a given place; i.e. "The House Rule here is that a Five-of-a-Kind beats a Royal Flush."

I

Ignorant End: The low end of a Straight.

Improve: To draw cards in Draw poker or to be dealt cards in Stud poker that increase the rank of the player's hand.

In: A player who has called all bets is considered in.

Inside Straight: A hand that is one card away from a Straight, but the card needed falls inside the Straight, as opposed to at the beginning or end. For example, a 4-5-7-8 is an inside straight, because the Six needed falls inside the cards held to complete the Straight. Also called Gutshot Straight.

J

Johnny: A Jack. Jacks are also referred to as Jake, Jacques or Knave.

Joker: Two or three extra cards included with a deck of playing cards; typically not used, but when they are, they are used as wild cards. See Bug.

K

Kibitzer: A spectator who is not only watching the game, but also commenting aloud as to what is happening in the game.

Kickers: (a) The two cards in a seven-card hand that are not part of the best five-card hand.

(b) The highest unpaired card in a player's hand is the player's kicker, and is used to determine the winner between tie hands.

King with the Battle Axe: The King of Diamonds.

Kick: To raise.

Kitty: A blind hand dealt face-down and not revealed until showdown. When used typically in Guts poker, the Kitty's hand must also be beat in addition to the other players' hands.

Knave: A Jack.

Knock: A player may knock the table with a fist to indicate a check.

L

Lay Down: To reveal a hand at showdown.

Leg: One game in a series of poker hands, where the rules require that a player win a number of times to collect the pot. In Double-Legged poker, for example, a player must win two hands (or legs) in order to collect the pot.

Legitimate Play: When a player bets in a way that corresponds accurately to his or her hand.

Light, To Be: To be short on the funds required to remain in the game. Some tables allow a player to state, for example, "I'm light, I owe the pot five dollars", meaning that the player owes five dollars to the player who wins the pot, unless that particular player happens to win. See Table Stakes.

Limit Poker: Poker played with fixed betting amounts.

Limp In: To call in late position.

Little Blind: The smaller compulsory ante in Hold 'Em paid by the first player to the left of the dealer. See Small Blind.

Little Ones: The lowest card in a player's hand and any that match it in the same hand. For example, if the lowest card in a player's hand is a Three, and that player has two of them, they are both the little ones. Typically designated in wild card games, such as Kings and Little Ones.

Live One: A poor player with plenty of money to lose. See Whale.

Lock: A hand that cannot lose. See Nuts.

Look: To call the final bet before showdown.

Loose: A style of play characterized by playing many hands. Loose-passive means a player who plays many hands but does not typically bet or raise. Loose-aggressive means a player who plays many hands and typically bets or raises.

Lowball: A type of game where the lowest hand at the table wins instead of the best hand. Players who do not count Straights and Flushes in Lowball count the A-2-3-4-5 as the best possible Lowball hand. See Bicycle Wheel. Players who count Straights and Flushes in Lowball count the A-2-3-4-6 as the best possible Lowball hand, as it is the worst possible poker hand. Also known as Low, Lowboy.

M

Make the Deck: To shuffle the deck.

Mark: A sucker. See Whale, Fish.

Marker: A disc used to indicate that an absent player owes money to the table.

Marked Deck: A deck with at least one card that has a marking on it identifying that card to cheating players.

Mechanic: A proficient cheat who can manipulate the deck.

Meet: To call.

Misdeal: A deal that must be started again because of an irregularity.

Monte Carlo: A specific type of Guts poker with three cards, including three-card Straights and Flushes.

Move In: To go all in.

Muck: (a) The collection of discarded hands that forms when a hand is played.
(b) To discard one's hand.

N

Natural: A term used in wild card games to describe the cards that make up a player's hand but are not wild cards.

No Fold'em Hold 'Em: A term used to describe a loose Texas Hold 'Em game where players will generally call most bets rather than fold.

No-Limit: A betting format where a player is allowed to bet as much money at any point as he has in front of him on the table. See Table Stakes.

Nuts: The best possible hand that a player can have, given the information that is available. In Community or Hold 'Em poker, that information is the shared community cards. In Stud poker, that information is the face-up cards that the player has showing. Also known as the Nut Hand.

PREPARING

BASICS

DRAW

STUD

GUTS

COMMUNITY

HOLD'EM

CASINO

NON-POKER

GLOSSARY

O

Off-Suit: Cards of different suits.
On-Tilt: A player who is betting loosely, generally because he or she is losing.
One-Eyed Jacks: The Jacks of Spades and Hearts.
Opening: The act performed by the player who initiates the betting round by starting it off with a bet. The opening bet is the sum of money with which that player opens the betting round.
Outside Straight: A hand that is one card away from a Straight, but the card needed falls at the beginning or end of the four cards held in order to complete the straight. For example, a 4-5-6-7 hand is an Outside Straight, because the cards needed to complete the straight, a Three or an Eight, fall before or after the cards held.
Outs: The possibility that would turn a losing hand into a winner.
Overcards: Any cards higher than the flop cards that would give top-pair.

P

Pack: A deck of cards.
Pair: Two cards of the same denomination.
Pass: To fold. Often incorrectly used to indicate a check.
Passive: A style of play characterized by checking and calling bets, rather than betting and raising. See also Aggressive, Loose, and Tight.
Pat, To Stay: The act of choosing not to take any new cards on the draw.
Picture Card: A face, or court card.
Pig, Calling: The act of trying to win both halves of the pot in a split-pot game. Used when players must declare what half of the pot they are going for (either high or low in High/Low games; either spade or best hand in Chicago games) and a player decides to try both. A player who calls pig must win both halves of the pot or wins nothing at all.
Pile: A stack of chips.
Pip: The symbols on a non-face card which indicate its rank.
Play Back: To re-raise.
Players Speak: The House Rule that each individual player is responsible for identifying his or her hand. What the player calls must indeed be in that player's hand for the call to count. A player that undercalls his or her hand has identified that hand as worse than it really is. See Cards Speak.
Pocket: Another term for hole cards.
Pocket Pair: Two hole cards of the same rank.
Poker Face: Adopted by more seasoned players, the ability to hide the strength or weakness of one's hand based on one's ability to retain composure. A player has no poker face if that player's hand can be read by other players.
Position: A player's proximity to the dealer. A player immediately to the left of the dealer is said to be in early position, while the dealer is considered to be in last position. Late position is generally advantageous as it allows a player to see how everybody else has bet before making a decision.
Position Bet: A bet based on that player's position at the table, as opposed to betting solely on the strength of one's hand. For example, betting in late position on an earlier betting round to discourage players from betting against you on later betting rounds.
Pot: The accumulated amount of money in the center of the table, awarded to the winner of the game.
Pot Limit: A game in which the maximum bet is equal to the size of the pot.
Pot Odds: A means to assess the value of an investment into a hand. Pot odds calculate the amount of money in the pot against the player's chances of winning the hand.
Pregnant Threes: An overdone Draw game where Threes, Sixes, and Nines are all wild.
Put Down: To fold.

Q

Quads: A Four-of-a-Kind.
Qualifier: In Draw, a given criteria that must be met by a player in order to either open the first betting round or win the pot. It is usually a specific ranked hand. For example, in the game Jacks or Better, Trips to Win, a pair of Jacks is the qualifier to open the first betting round, and a Three-of-a-Kind is the qualifier to win the pot.

R

Rag: In Stud poker, when a player is dealt a card that does not help the hand at all. For example, being one card away from a Flush and being dealt a card of a different suit that does not even pair up with any cards currently held.

Railbird: A one-time player, now a broke spectator.

Rainbow: A hand containing at least one card of all four suits. The nemesis of a Flush.

Raise: The act of matching all of the bets that have been previously made, then adding yet another bet for all other players to match.

Rake: The commission on a pot taken by the house.

Rank: The number or hierarchy of a single card. For example, in Queen of Spades, Spades makes reference to the suit, while Queen makes reference to the rank.

Rap: To knock the table to indicate a check.

Read: To read a player means to look for physical tendencies or beyond their poker face to discern whether their hand is true to what they are representing.

Re-Buy: To re-enter a tournament for an additional entry fee.

Red: The color of poker chip most often used to represent the middle denomination of money, typically two times the table's ante and/or minimum bet.

Representing: Based on evidence that other players can see (face-up cards in Stud, community cards in Hold 'Em), a players are said to represent a certain hand based on the way they are betting. They may or may not actually have the hand that they are representing.

Re-raise: The act of adding another raise to an already raised bet.

Riffle: To shuffle one's chips.

River: (a) In Hold 'Em, the last community card turned face-up.
(b) More loosely in Stud, the last card dealt face-down to each player.

Rivered, To Be: A player who loses a hand to another player who completed a better hand on the last card of the round, known as the River, is said to have been rivered.

Rock: An extremely tight player.

Roll: To turn a card face up.

Royal Flush: A-K-Q-J-10 of the same suit. The best possible hand in all non-wild card games.

Run: (a) A straight.
(b) A streak of good cards.

Running Bad: On a losing streak.

Running Good: On a winning streak.

Rush: A player who is playing against the odds due to a streak of good cards is said to be on a rush.

S

Sandbag: To check a strong hand with the intention of raising or re-raising any bets. See Check-raising.

Satellite: A small-stakes tournament whose winner is granted entry into a bigger tournament.

School: A group of players in a regular game.

Seeing: Matching a previous bet, or all previously made bets, in order to stay in the game. When a betting round reaches a player, that player can see and call (does not bump with any more money) or see and raise (bumps with more money).

Set: Three-of-a-Kind, or Trips.

Set A Player In: To bet as much as an opponent has left in the hopes of forcing him or her to go all-in.

Shill: A casino employee who plays with house money to make enough players to complete a game.

Short Stack: The player with the least amount of chips.

Showdown: The end of the hand, and point where it is determined by players which of them wins the pot. The showdown is the act of all players remaining in the game showing their hands in full to the table.

Shuffle: To mix the cards before dealing.

Side-Pot: A separate pot contested by players when another player is all-in.

Skin: (a) To draw a card.
(b) To cheat.

PREPARING

BASICS

DRAW

STUD

GUTS

COMMUNITY

HOLD'EM

CASINO

NON-POKER

GLOSSARY

Slowplay: The act of under-betting a good hand, to avoid scaring other players into folding early. It is used to build the size of the pot without revealing too much about one's hand.

Small Blind: The smaller of the two compulsory antes. See Little Blind.

Snake Eyes: A pair of Aces.

Softplay: To let a friend off easy in a hand.

Soixante-neuf: French for sixty-nine, an expression for when a player's two cards showing are a six and a nine.

Split Pot: (a) Any game where the pot is split between more than one player, used in high/low and Chicago games.

(b) A pot that needs to be divided between players with identical hands.

Squeeze: To look slowly at one's hole cards without removing them from the table. The common method by which most players examine their cards in Hold 'Em.

Stack: The pile of chips in front of a player.

Stacking the Deck: A dealer purposely arranges the cards in his or her favor while shuffling.

Standoff: A hand which ends in a tie. The pot is divided evenly.

Stand Pat: To decline drawing cards when given the opportunity.

Stay: To call a hand without raising. Also known as Stick.

Steal: A late position bluff intended to take the pot from a table of weak hands.

Steaming: To play badly, and loosely. See On-Tilt.

Straight: Five consecutive cards. Beats Three-of-a-Kind, but loses to a Flush.

Straight Flush: Five consecutive cards of the same suit. Beats any hand but a higher Straight Flush.

Straight Poker: Usually referring to Draw poker, means that there are no wild cards and no special rules or stipulations.

Street: In Stud and Hold 'Em poker, a round of one card dealt to each player. For example, the fifth card dealt to each player is called Fifth Street.

String Bet: A bet in which player puts some chips into a pot, then reaches for more to raise a previous bet without declaring a raise before calling. This an illegal bet.

Stuck: Losing.

Stud: Any game where each player has some cards dealt face-down and some face-up that all other players can see. Likewise, each player can see the face-up cards of the other players.

Suicidal King: The King of Hearts, named such as it appears he is piercing his own head with his sword.

Suited Cards: Cards of the same suit in one hand. A player with enough suited cards is likely pursuing a Flush.

Sweeten the Pot: To raise.

T

Table: (a) The surface on which the game is played.

(b) The group of players at the table.

Table Stakes: The House Rule that no player can bet (or lose) any amount that is not in front of him or her and on the table. In other words, a player cannot put additional money on the table in the middle of a hand in order to be able to bet more. This is more often cited in No-Limit poker, where players who wish to call a bet but do not have enough money to cover the bets is permitted to go All-in, remain in the game, but win only as much money as they were able to call.

Tapped: To go broke. Also known as, Tap City.

Tap Out: To bet all of one's chips.

Tells: Signals from a particular player that help the observer discern what kind of a hand that player has. For example, biting one's bottom lip whenever dealt a good hand, or lighting up a cigarette whenever dealt a bad hand.

Three-Flush: Three cards of the same suit.

Three-of-a-Kind: Three cards of the same denomination. Beats Two Pair, but loses to a Straight.

Three Pair: A comical reference to a seven-card hand containing three Pairs. Because a poker hand only consists of five cards, there is no such thing as Three Pairs even though it is what that player was dealt. The player may hold three Pairs, but only two count.

Tight: A style of play characterized by much folding and not playing many hands. Tight-passive means a player who does not play many hands, and does not typically bet or raise when playing a hand. Tight-aggressive means a player who does not play many hands, but typically bets or raises when hands are played.

Trips: A Three-of-a-Kind. See Set.

Trey: A Three.

Trump: Rarely used in poker. A card of the designated trump suit beats any other card played except a higher card of the trump suit.

Tugboat: Expression for a Full House made up of low cards. For example, a Full House of three Twos and two Fives.

Turn: The fourth community card dealt face-up in Texas Hold 'Em.

Two Pairs: A hand containing two pairs. Beats a Pair, but loses to Three-of-a-Kind.

U

Under-Raise: To raise less than the previous bet if a player is going all-in.

Under the Gun: The player who is the first to bet is said to be under the gun.

Up-Card: An open or exposed card.

W

Whale: A poor player with plenty of money to lose.

Wheel: A-2-3-4-5. The lowest hand in Lowball. See Bicycle Wheel.

Whipsawed: Seated between two players who are constantly raising and re-raising each other's bets. This places the player in the position of having to choose whether or not to compete with the two players. Also called being Sandwiched.

White: The color of poker chip most often used to represent the smallest denomination of money, typically the table's ante and/or minimum bet. The logic behind this is that store-bought poker chips typically contain more white chips than red or blue.

Wild Card: A card designated by the dealer before the deal that, if dealt to a player, can be made into any card of any suit that player chooses. For example, if the dealer calls Twos as wild, then any player with a Two can make that Two any card of any suit, even to complete a Straight or a Flush.

Wired: Two paired hole cards. See Back to Back.

Y

Yard: One hundred dollars.

Z

Zombie: A player who shows absolutely no emotion during game play, making him or her virtually impossible to read.

PREPARING

BASICS

DRAW

STUD

GUTS

COMMUNITY

HOLD'EM

CASINO

NON-POKER

GLOSSARY

About the Authors

Marc Wortman is the founder of HomePoker. com, and has been collecting and contributing information to the home poker world through his website for over six years.

Joel Krass is a managing partner of Home-Poker.com and writes as Joel the Poker Scribe for HomePoker.com, answering questions on home poker via email and at the HomePoker.com discussion forum.

About HomePoker.com

HomePoker.com is devoted to enriching the experience of the home gamer by offering community, information, products and services. Currently the top-ranked poker web site on Google, it is host to over 2400 unique poker players daily, offering a wide range of free information on the game of poker. HomePoker. com has detailed information on strategy, game variations, book and software reviews, discussion forums as well as an online poker chip store.

BradyGAMES Staff

Publisher
David Waybright

Editor-In-Chief
H. Leigh Davis

Director of Marketing
Steve Escalante

Marketing Manager
Janet Eshenour

Creative Director
Robin Lasek

Licensing Manager
Mike Degler

Assistant Marketing Manager
Susie Nieman

Team Coordinator
Stacey Beheler

Credits

Senior Development Editor
Ken Schmidt

Book Designer
Tim Amrhein

ISBN: 0-7440-0508-6

Library of Congress Catalog No.: 2004116384
Printing Code: The rightmost double-digit number is the year of the book's printing; the rightmost single-digit number is the number of the book's printing. For example, 04-1 shows that the first printing of the book occurred in 2004.
07 06 05 04   4 3 2 1
Manufactured in the United States of America.

Limits of Liability and Disclaimer of Warranty:
THE AUTHOR AND PUBLISHER MAKE NO WARRANTY OF ANY KIND, EXPRESSED OR IMPLIED, WITH REGARD TO THESE PROGRAMS OR THE DOCUMENTATION CONTAINED IN THIS BOOK. THE AUTHOR AND PUBLISHER SPECIFICALLY DISCLAIM ANY WARRANTIES OF MERCHANTABILITY OR FITNESS FOR A PARTICULAR PURPOSE. THE AUTHOR AND PUBLISHER SHALL NOT BE LIABLE IN ANY EVENT FOR INCIDENTAL OR CONSEQUENTIAL DAMAGES IN CONNECTION WITH, OR ARISING OUT OF, THE FURNISHING, PERFORMANCE, OR USE OF THESE PROGRAMS.